CROMLECHS AND CAIRNS
in northern Wales

CROMLECHS AND CAIRNS
in northern Wales

by

MICHAEL SENIOR

936.29

ISBN: 1-84527-049-5

Cover illustration: Cromlech Ystum Cegid Isaf
Cover design: Sian Parri

First published in 2006 by
Gwasg Carreg Gwalch, 12 Iard yr Orsaf, Llanrwst,
Wales LL26 0EH.
Phone: 01492 642031   Fax: 01492 641502
e-mail: books@carreg-gwalch.co.uk
Website: www.carreg-gwalch.co.uk

CONTENTS

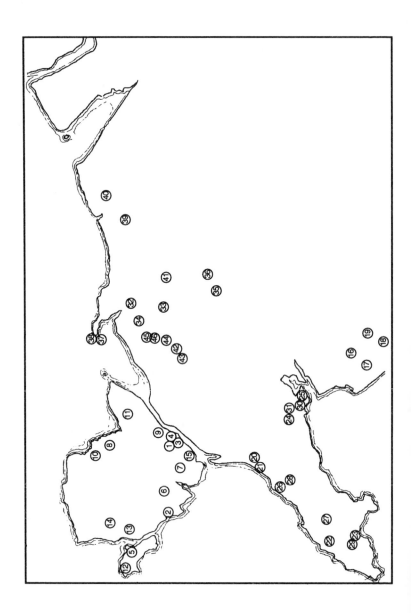

Anglesey
1. Bryn Celli Ddu
2. Barclodiad y Gawres
3. Bryn yr Hen Bobl
4. Plas Newydd
5. Trefignath
6. Din Dryfol
7. Bodowyr
8. Pant y Saer
9. Tŷ Newydd
10. Lligwy
11. Hen Drefor
12. Garn, Holyhead Mountain
13. Prysaddfed
14. Bedd Branwen
15. Garn, Bryn Siencyn

Ardudwy
16. Gwen Einion
17. Dyffryn Ardudwy

18. Carneddau Hengwm
19. Cors y Gedol

Llŷn/Eifionydd
20. Penarth
21. Bach Wen
22. Mynydd Cefnamwlch
23. Tan y Muriau
24. Rhoslan
25. Cist Cerrig
26. Yr Eifl
27. Carn Fadrun
28. Carnguwch
29. Mynydd Rhiw
30. Coetan Arthur
31. Ystum Cegid Isaf

Conwy Valley and Great Orme
32. Allor Moloch

33. Porth Llwyd
34. Maen y Bardd
35. Capel Garmon
36. Maen Pebyll
37. Llety'r Filiast
38. Gogarth
39. Tyddyn Bleiddyn
40. Gop
41. Mwdwl Eithin

Carneddau
42. Carnedd Llywelyn
43. Carnedd Dafydd
44. Carnedd y Saeson
45. Drosgl
46. Drum

AUTHOR'S PREFACE

If this book cures anyone of a tendency to be patronising about our fellow countrymen of the very distant past it will have been worth writing. To speak or think of them as if they are assumed to be primitive or naïve, simply because they lived so long ago, is to adopt a notion of development which will be shown here, I hope, to be fallacious. Certainly they did not have the advantage of our technology; so much greater is the achievement of their skills. Indeed it might be said they do not seem to have needed these mechanical aids. It is perhaps we who lack their advantages.

Consider: could you, even with the aid of a JCB, raise a several-ton boulder some five feet off the ground and rest it there on the points of three or four slender upright stones? In such a way, that is, that it would stay in place for at least five thousand years? Nor should it be implied that the thinking behind such acts was unsophisticated, for instance by portraying them in our imagination as being driven by superstitious beliefs in imaginary gods. Do we not, now, erect memorials to deal with the thoughts and feelings which surround the dead?

It will be shown here (I hope) that the people who achieved these wonders were far from primitive. Nor will it do to shelter behind the notion that we know too little about them to give them the level of understanding that we award ourselves. I hope it will be clear by the end of this book that we know, in fact, a great deal about them. But even had it been the case that all we knew of them was what they left behind, then the cromlechs and the cairns or northern Wales would, by themselves, be sufficient to require our respect.

As we move around northern Wales in this book and confront these proud monuments in their ancient settings you may well begin to think that respect is too weak a notion, verging perhaps again on the patronising. Awe might be a better word. Myself I have come to feel that not only were these people not inferior to ourselves, but that, if flights of imagination, commitment to the value of ideas, and the strength and determination involved in expressing these intellectual concepts – if all these should be accounted positive qualities, these people were at least to that extent superior.

Michael Senior
Glan Conwy, April 2006.

To the memory of
Elanwy Ash

INTRODUCTION
TWO SUBJECTS – ONE THEME

This is a book about two distinct subjects, but with a common background. Cromlechs and cairns are, as we see them now, different types of structure, of different periods and associated with recognisably different social cultures. Some one and a half thousand years separate the earliest cromlechs from the Bronze Age cairns (though there are elements of transition, and so of continuity). We know that they were all concerned with means of disposal of the dead. The theme which runs through their chronology, and so connects them, it that of the human attitude to death.

Let me to start with clarify the basic subjects of this book. Cromlech is term which comes from two Welsh words, *crom*, the feminine of *crwm*, meaning 'bent', and *llech*, a feminine noun meaning 'stone' (now more particularly meaning 'slate'). It has been used by some to mean 'stone circle', but here at least its meaning is fixed. It refers to the form of chamber tomb which consists of a horizontal stone supported by uprights. This form is known in France by the Breton name 'dolmen', from *tol*, a table, and *men*, stone, graphically giving the description 'stone table'. and this term is used in general here as the equivalent of cromlech, and more particularly in Wales as one type of burial chamber, as in the term 'portal dolmen'.

The term cairn comes from the Welsh, and Gaelic, word *carn*, meaning a heap. It occurs in Wales in another form, *carnedd*, and the dictionary makes no distinction between the two forms. It may be (though decisions on this are hard to find) that the difference is equivalent to our English suffix '-ful' – *carnedd* thus expressing, as near as we can get, a 'cairn-ful'.

It is established that both types of prehistoric structure known by these terms (cromlechs and cairns) were to do with burial, since burials have usually been found within them. We shall deal in the first chapter with the types, and the distribution, of the two forms. Here it might simply be said that there are some fifty of these tombs in the area being dealt with here, and very many more cairns, so that we may describe in detail the best examples of the various types of the former, but can only take examples – the most prominent, and the most investigated – of the latter.

The first chapter will review the actual subject matter we have before us, the range and type of artefact. In considering this we will be aware of the differences between the two types, cromlechs and cairns, and the change of attitudes which they exemplify. Later we shall consider how this change came about, when we look into the details of life in the Late Stone Age, and the Early Bronze Age, in chapter five. Here it is enough to note that a change undoubtedly did take place, a change (whatever it was) which manifested itself in the modes of memorial. It is because of that change that we have two subjects. It is because the two contrasting forms addressed the same dilemmas that we have one theme.

I intend, as I have done before in works describing our other ancient artefacts, the standing stones and the Iron Age hillforts, to set these examples which are before us in a wider context, in order the better to understand them. Thus the second chapter will consider the phylogenesis of the form, no less than the history of the means of disposal of the dead – and hence, we may presume, the means of confronting and controlling the thoughts and speculations to which the dead give rise.

Pursuing the programme of setting the features in their context, the third chapter will trace the route by which they came here, from the distant origins of their forms in eastern Europe. We shall then be in a better position (in chapter four) to view our examples of these forms in detail, and the way they relate to our landscape.

ONE
PERMANENT MEMORIALS

At first glance they are just old mysterious structures. We tend to assume that whatever the motive for building them was, it was so long ago and under such different circumstances that we shall never understand it. So we lump them together, as all strange things from the past.

It is only when you look a little closer that it becomes apparent that they are in fact, amongst themselves, different. A closer look still will reveal that some of them have distinct things in common; then suddenly they begin to fall into groups.

It seems it was the Reverend W. C. Lukis who first produced a systematic classification of prehistoric burial chambers, in 1864. Lukis was a student of megaliths of all types, in Britain and in Europe as a whole. He proposed that megalithic tombs fell into two groups: simple chambers, characterised by a single roofing stone; and complex chambers, with what he called a 'covered way' leading to them. Needless to say this admirably clear distinction has proved inadequate to more modern scholars.

Lukis was soon considered to have left things out. Oscar Montelius, a Swedish archaeologist, produced his improvement on the original scheme, in 1876. There were, Montelius opined, not two but three distinguishable groups: simple chambers; rectangular or polygonal chambers approached by a passage; and elongated rectangular chambers with no passage. In later terms these three groups came to be known as 'dolmens', 'passage graves', and 'gallery graves'. Glyn Daniel (in the book *The Megalith Builders of Western Europe*, from which this information is gleaned), proposes refinement of the first form into three sub-species: round, simple, single chambers; polygonal chambers; and rectangular single chambers. Finally he ends up with seven sub-categories, but thankfully these are grouped under the three main headings which we started with, now better termed as: **single chambers, passage graves,** and **gallery graves.**

The tombs may be further distinguished by whether they are 'open' or 'closed', the first being potentially entered by removal of a blocking deposit, in the case of the second entry being impossible, access to the chamber deliberately obstructed by an orthostat – a technical term, used apparently only in the study of megaliths, meaning a large stone set on edge. This phenomenon, the blocked entrance, is a frequent characteristic in cases we will be considering. It belongs to a type known as the 'portal dolmen', (of which there are, strangely, none in Anglesey), in which the entrance is a developed feature, which Frances Lynch, in *Prehistoric Wales*, interprets as "the point of contact between the worlds of the living and the dead".

In the portal dolmen, as we shall amply see, the tall portals are a distinguishing element, but appear to be non-functional. The fine examples at **Dyffryn Ardudwy**, on the Harlech coast, will convey the essential features of this form. Here Early Neolithic pottery was found in association with the closure of the portal, making it seem likely that the closing material was part of the original design.

Portal dolmens are found on both sides of the Irish Sea, in Cornwall as well as Wales, and in west and south-east Ireland. They consist of a single chamber, and a high closed entrance in the form of an H, somewhat like a house of cards. The slab across the entrance is often shown to be designed specifically as a closing feature, as (in some cases) if it were removed the house of cards would collapse. Such tombs occur in locally dense distribution, between 35 and 50 of them in Wales and south-west England, characteristically located on lower ground which is at present farmland – hence usually disturbed, leading to a lack of finds. Frances Lynch is of the opinion (this time in *Megalithic Tombs and Long Barrows in Britain*) that the blocked entrance would not entirely prevent re-use: "It would usually be possible to insert bones, if not bodies, over the closing slab but there is no positive evidence of the original burial ritual in this group".

We will come to this business of the chambers' use shortly. Meanwhile I should mention the other common form of burial structure in Wales, the passage grave. These occur in two main groups, in relatively isolated examples. There are seven apparently early examples in West Wales and in Anglesey, and several of a probably later date in north-western Wales. **Bryn Celli Ddu**, in Anglesey, is regarded by Glyn Daniel as "the best example of a passage grave in England and Wales". **Barclodiad y Gawres**, also in Anglesey, is an unusual specimen of this form, in that (Daniel says) this site "is the only cruceiform passage grave known to me in southern Britain".

Daniel classified the types by distinguishing the forms of their chambers, but it is not the only way possible. W. F. Grimes, who wrote a paper on the subject in 1936, distinguished them by their overall shape. On the assumption that all such tombs were originally covered by mounds, he distinguished between those which would **Maen y Bardd** above the Dyffryn Conwy (*dyffryn:* valley.

It is perhaps a less satisfactory form of classification, but it does draw our attention to the mound, or cairn, as a feature of the megaliths.

Frances Lynch, in the book last referred to, says that the mound is thought to have been a universal feature of the tombs. It does not follow, she says, that it was primary: "the stage at which it was built may still be a subject of discussion". Mounds have been found without burials: in Wiltshire, for instance, where have had round mounds and those covered by long ones. Passage graves in round mounds include **Bryn Celli Ddu** and **Barclodiad y Gawres.** Long cairns are to be found in connection with the tombs at **Capel Garmon** where bones would have been well preserved in the chalk. This "suggests that the mound was gaining significance in its own right". Although the cairns with which we shall also be concerned in this book were demonstrably for the purpose of burial, this attention to the cairn structure as of symbolic significance (perhaps by association with the dead) is of interest to us as a link between our two subjects.

Cairns are less complex, of course, than chamber tombs. We shall in due course be making comparisons and distinctions between structures known as either cairns or barrows, which get divided into 'rectangular', 'gallery', and 'long'.

Both types of structure, cromlechs and cairns, show recognisable patterns in their distribution, but these anyway result from the basic land-form of northern Wales. In Anglesey, where there are between twenty and thirty chamber tombs remaining – opinions vary: Wheeler has fifty, Grimes seventeen – they avoid completely the marshy centre, and cluster mainly around the cultivatable land bordering the Menai Strait. The barrows (or cairns) here are fewer, broadly circling the island, and occur most frequently in connection with its rivers. In the central area of northern Wales and in Llŷn the tombs do not occur in the mountainous heartland at all, but sporadically around the coastal plain and in the Dyffryn Conwy, and only appear to cluster in groups on the southern coast of Llŷn, above Tremadog Bay. The cairns, on the other hand, suggesting a contrasting way of life, seem to seek mountain tops, the higher the better, and occur in massive quantities in the eastern reaches of the Carnedd range. A further band of chamber tombs stretches down the coast south of Harlech. Safe landings and fertile farmland seem, at first glance, to be the main concerns of the tomb builders; such as are any distance inland are up river valleys. The cairn builders rather reach out to uncultivated places. However, Grimes notes that there are no tombs along the coast of central Cardiff Bay: they start again, plentifully, in Pembrokeshire. He speculates that the cause of this might be the existence, prior to an inundation, of "a belt of low-lying land in front of the present coast", preventing settlement. Maybe some lie under what is now the sea?

As Grimes notes the low-lying locations of most of the tombs – **Maen y Bardd** is an obvious exception – means that "many of the sites must have been well below the natural tree level". He speculates, and we must regard this as being inevitable, that they were sited on already cleared areas, and therefore that the forest was already giving way to farming, even at this very remote period. The cairns, on the other hand, favouring barren hilltops, were sited above or at the edge of the tree level, particularly where this was depressed, as in the northern Carneddau, by the salt-laden sea wind.

There are exceptions, but most of them lie between 1,000 and 1,500 feet; almost all in fact, in our area, above 500. Those on the two Carneddau themselves are an exception the other way, both sited at over 3,400 feet. It is known that the climate was at that time better than now, being dry and warm, and so led to the thinning downwards of the forest edge. There is no direct suggestion, however, that the people who buried their dead on mountain tops actually lived at this altitude, though since we do not know where else they may have lived, their dwellings evidently being light and temporary and having left no trace, they may have done so.

The cairns are not mere heaps of stone, but were constructed according to certain principles, just like the chambers. At their centre lies the burial, now in the form of an urn containing cremated bones, protected in an elaborately built stone box, known to archaeologists as a 'cist' (from the Welsh word for chest). This was massively covered over, only to be revealed millennia later by robbers or antiquarians, but we have to remember, of course, that so were the larger boxes which we marvel at in their stripped, skeletal form. Indeed the fact that one type is now still covered is misleading. It does not means that the covering element was any more important in these cases. Its survival is probably simply due to the striking difference in location we have already mentioned. One type of monument is in present-day as well as ancient farmland; the other on remote and untouched mountains. Hence the mounds of Stone Age tombs have gone, probably robbed for the construction of walls and buildings and cleared to facilitate cultivation.

The Bronze Age cists were usually some three to five feet long and around two foot wide. Some of them are reminiscent in style of their predecessor tombs, prompting the writers of the Royal Commission Inventory to comment that the "traditions of megalith builders are perhaps preserved in the massive capstones and side slabs of some of these cists". In many cases the boundaries of the covering mound were then laid out, in the form of a kerb of slabs laid on edge, or sometimes a revetment, like a low dry-stone wall. The cairn has in most cases collapsed across this border, and there is in fact no reason to think that it was ever completely contained within it. In some cases what amounts to a ring of uprights ties these mounds in form with stone circles

The average diameter of the circular mounds is 32 feet, but this covers a considerable variation in bulk. There are cairns, such as **Carnguwch** in Llŷn, which are more than ten foot high, and over 100 feet wide. There are some on the slopes of **Tal y Fan** which are so low and indistinct that some specialists have queried their status as cairns at all.

Perhaps also due to their location and the consequent retention of their mounds, the Bronze Age cairns have been less disturbed than the Stone Age chambers, so that we know rather more about their purpose and their builders. Even in the undisturbed chambers, Glyn Daniel remarks that the quantity of artefacts is small, indicating perhaps that grave goods were not a concern of that early time. We shall be considering the nature of the people and their way of life later, but it would be perverse not to remark at the outset on what we know of the uses of these monuments.

Although there was a time when antiquarians considered that they might be temples, there is now no doubt among the experts that the primary use of all these structures was sepulchral. This does not rule out, they are quick to point out, ritual activity in connection with the burials, nor rule out subsequent veneration of the sites. At Pentre Ifan, in Pembrokeshire, it was found that the long cairn which once surrounded the monument was added, together with a stone façade, after the chamber was closed, so that, as Frances Lynch considers, "the tomb retained an active ceremonial role" which was "no longer primarily concerned with burials". Excavation has also revealed signs of fires within or in the forecourts of several of the chambers, and some confusion arises in the cases where bones were burnt in such ritual fires. These, it is clear, are not cases of cremation: the bones in Stone Age burials were normally inhumed in the chambers in their solid state.

Something must be said now about this which will concern us later, since it throws some light on these distant people's attitude towards the dead. They were enclosed in the great stone chambers as bones, rather than as individual bodies. This is in stark contrast to the habits of the later cairn-builders, since in those cists were the burnt remains of usually one, sometimes two, individuals.

The number of bodies from which bones are found, in the undisturbed and excavated chambers, is greater than the number of corpses that could have been placed in the chamber together. Such was found to be the case at the excavated tomb at **Pant y Saer** in Anglesey. This fact (observed elsewhere, such as at Mesara, in Crete, and St. Eugène, near Carcassonne, where the remains of some 300 copses were found) gives rise to a selection of alternative theories. A related fact, which may help in explanation, is that the bones in most burial chambers are scattered around in, as Daniel puts it, a state of confusion. Some appear to have been deliberately broken, a fact not yet satisfactorily explained. Moreover when any attempt is made to reconstruct the skeletons it is found that some bits are missing. "Thus it is," says Daniel, "that the estimates of the numbers of people buried in the tombs varies according to the bones on which they are based." It would seem then either that the bodies have been allowed to decay elsewhere, and that the tombs are ossuaries rather than the sites of primary burial; or that they were re-opened to receive fresh burials, over perhaps a long period of time, and that the remains of former burials were pushed to one side and if it were necessary to make adequate room chucked out.

The second hypothesis receives some support from the fact that occasionally a body is found intact, sometimes set apart from the heaps of bones. This might represent the very latest burial, before the tomb was abandoned. It must be said that there is evidence that some tombs were closed permanently on construction, and therefore only used once, though these still contain the remains of large numbers of people; but the vast majority of chamber tombs in England and Wales were open, in the sense that they could have been re-used.

We may, then, posit a tentative theory of the process of use of the tombs. Bodies were stored in temporary resting places until enough had accumulated to justify re-opening the tomb. Room was then made for them inside. Some ceremonies took place, involving the use of fire. The tomb was then re-closed. And so on for some hundreds of years.

The distribution of the structures, and their location in cultivatable land, fits a theory that they were the repositories for the ancestral bones of an extended family, probably a farming unit settled on the adjoining land. Family resemblances were noted in the early excavations, and Frances Lynch several times remarks on evidence that the skeletons belonged to a single family group. It is thus convenient, she says, to think of the tomb as being a family church or vault. One thing that is clear is that the individuals there buried are not in any way distinguished, one from another. There are men, women and children, in an undifferentiated muddle. "This evidence" (says Lynch) "suggests that the mass of bone is important, not as a series of individuals, but as a group of anonymous ancestors amongst whom any distinctions of wealth or status have been obliterated."

This is a system quite unlike that of the subsequent Bronze Age, and in due course we must consider what this tells us about the people, and what else of that we can infer from other sources.

Of course the change in burial habits has a double, and contradictory, effect on our state of knowledge of the people. By burying them with grave goods (a habit practically unknown to their predecessors) the Bronze Age people tell us something about the wealth and status of the deceased. On the other hand by cremating them first they deprive us of any detailed knowledge of the individuals themselves. Cremation was found to be a practice in earlier tombs in Spain and France, and is frequent in Ireland. But there is little evidence of it in Britain until the onset of the Bronze Age.

The problem with the dating of these periods is not just that finds in the earlier tombs are scarce, but is more of a general problem common to all archaeological dating: how do we know whether something found is primary, in the sense of being contemporary with the original structure, or secondary, as having been added to it later? The probability is that the tombs were used for several centuries, and such slight finds as there have been (including charcoal, which can be radiocarbon dated) may be from any period of their use.

The absence of metal in the chamber tombs led early antiquarians to label them Stone Age, and in so far as such categorisation is still accepted we cannot disagree. Radiocarbon dating has been available since the 1950's, and enables us to place them between 4000 and 3500 BC. The process of transition, as we shall see, appears to have been gradual, the practices of cremation and inhumation at one time co-existing. The megalithic chambers became degraded (as Glyn Daniel puts it) until, as in the case of **Caerdyni,** near Cricieth, it amounted "to what should properly be termed a cist". There is no evidence for the continuation of the full megalithic style after 3000 BC.

One feature which is sometimes thought not to have been original is the rock-art very rarely found in connection with the burial chambers. This takes two forms, the small depressions termed 'cup-marks', over seventy of which appear on the surface of stones forming the burial chamber at **Clynnog;** and spirals and geometric lines, such as those found at **Bryn Celli Ddu** and **Barclodiad y Gawres.** Glyn Daniel thinks that some of these may be Bronze Age or indeed more recent.

These paradigm examples are sites which we will visit. The two famous Anglesey monuments are fine examples of passage graves, while that at **Capel Garmon,** ostensibly of the same form, contains idiosyncratic features which link it with tombs elsewhere. The portal dolmen form is well represented by the large structures at **Dyffryn Ardudwy,** and so too, though in a more ruined state, is the long-cairned **Carneddau Hengwm** at Dyffryn nearby. It would seem natural to pick **Maen y Bardd**, above the Conwy valley, as a specimen of the single-chambered type; yet it has been argued that this is the chamber of a passage grave of which the mound was never completed. So not all the styles and forms are unequivocally distinct, at least in their present form. The large double monument in the park of **Plas Newydd**, for instance, is either a pair of simple chambers, one added to the other, or an unusual form of passage grave. Anglesey also has a number of examples of yet another type, the gallery grave: **Trefignath**, for instance, at Holyhead, and (though in ruins) **Din Dryfol** at Aberffraw.

For many of these well-known sites we have the views of noted authorities to assist us with our visits. Inspecting some lesser specimens as well will help to fill out our understanding of the general forms.

TWO

THE BURIAL OF THE DEAD

We must suppose that some five hundred years after the Trojan War, when Homer wrote, the habit of disposal of the dead was as he describes it in the Odyssey. If so it accords quite accurately with something which had been going on in Britain and Ireland for some two thousand years by c. 750 BC:

> They made a pyre a hundred feet in length and breadth, and with sorrowful hearts laid the corpse on top ... Achilles wept as he burnt his comrade's bones, moving round the pyre on leaden feet with many a deep groan ... Then, with tears on their cheeks, they collected the white bones of their gentle comrade in a golden vase, closed it with a double seal of fat ... Next they designed his barrow by laying down a ring of stone revetments round the pyre. Then they fetched earth and piled it up inside.

As Achilles does for Patroculus, so Priam instructs the Trojans how to dispose of the dead Hector:

> It took them nine days to gather the huge quantity of wood required. But when the dawn of the tenth day brought light to the world, they carried out the gallant Hector with tears on their cheeks, laid his body on top of the pyre and set fire to the wood ... Then Hector's brothers and comrades-in-arms collected his white bones, lamenting as they worked with many a big tear

running down their cheeks. They took the bones, wrapped them in soft purple cloths and put them in a golden chest. This chest they quickly lowered into a hollow grave, which they covered with a layer of large stones closely set together. Then, hastily, they made the barrow ...

Homer later describes Achilles' own funeral rites in the same way:

> ... on the eighteenth day we committed you to the flames, with a rich sacrifice of fatted sheep and shambling cattle at your pyre ... When the sacred flames had consumed you, we gathered your white bones at dawn, Achilles, and laid them by in unmixed wine and oil. Then your mother gave us a golden urn ... In this your white bones lie ... Over them all, we soldiers of the mighty Argive force built up a great and glorious mound, on a foreland jutting out over the broad waters of the Hellespont, so that it might be seen far out at sea by the sailors of today and future ages.

The mound is an important feature. As the soul of Achilles had earlier been reported to have said to the soul of Agamemnon in *The Oddyssey*, the latter was unfortunate not to have died at Troy on the field of battle, as 'then the whole nation would have joined in building you a mound'.

It is an irony that these most explicit descriptions of the burial habits of the Achaeans and Trojans at Troy are apparently an anachronism on Homer's part. Cremation was not practised either in Greece or Asia Minor at the time of the Trojan War; but as already mentioned, we must suppose that it was at the time Homer wrote, some 500 years after the events a style occasionally enlivened by authorial comment helps to overcome (as critics and readers have noted) the danger that the material might be dry or dull.

Similar practices may be attributed to the Anglo-Saxons:

Then the people of the Geats prepared a pyre for him on the earth, unstinted, hung about with helmets, battle-shields and bright coats of mail, as his wish was. In the midst the lamenting heroes then laid down the famous prince, the beloved lord. Then on the mount the fighting-men began to kindle the greatest of funeral-fires; wood-smoke climbed up, black over the blaze, roaring flame mingled with weeping ... until it had broken the bone frame ... Then the people of the Weders constructed on the promontory a mound which was high and broad, to be seen far and near by those voyaging across the waves, and in ten days had built up a monument to the man renowned in battle; they surrounded the remains of the fire with a rampart, the finest that the most skilful men could devise. In the barrow they placed rings and brooches ...

Had the author of *Beowulf* been reading Homer? The poem was written about the year 1000, possibly from an earlier, perhaps eighth century text, but concerns itself with events of the first part of the sixth century. He may have intended the burial customs he described to be archaic. Cremation was a practice of the Anglo-Saxons before they came to Britain and during the early part of their settlement here. Urns and brooches feature in the burials of both

British and continental Germanic people in the fifth century. It is interesting that inhumation was practised here at the same time, and gradually came to dominate, though cremation went on until early Christian times.

Almost as strong a feature as the pyre and the mound in these early descriptions of burial rites is the mourning. One might be tempted to think that in early times when death came soon and randomly, our ancestors would have been hardened to bereavement. We are lucky to have the evidence of the early literature, and this early literature makes it clear that it was the mourning, the sense of loss, that provided the prime motive for formal sepulchral ceremonies. Those tears that ran down the cheeks of the ancient Greeks and Anglo-Saxons were as much a part of their funeral ceremonies as the setting up of stones and the heaping of mounds. They find an echo in the earliest literary evidence we have that deals with confronting bereavement: *The Epic of Gilgamesh.*

The Epic of Gilgamesh, written on clay tablets in Mesopotamia during the second millennium BC, probably about 1,500 years before the time of Homer, makes the experience of bereavement into a central theme, and only deals incidentally with the actual business of disposal. This is of interest because, although it was written in a different part of the world, it is direct testimony of the thoughts of the people themselves who were living when our later prehistoric monuments were being built: 'Bitterly Gilgamesh wept for his friend Enkidu; he wandered over the wilderness as a hunter, he roamed over the plains; in his bitterness he cried, "How can I rest, how can I be at peace? Despair is in my heart." A fear of death and its powers of obliteration comes to possess Gilgamesh, and he goes on a quest to find everlasting life. First, however, there is the very real problem of separation: '... the next day also, in the first light, Gilgamesh lamented; seven days and seven nights he wept for Enkidu, until the worm fastened on him. Only then he gave him up to the earth ...' No monuments surround the body (though Gilgamesh has a statue made), but Gilgamesh, through a process of reluctance to accept the fact of separation, has to recognise that the decomposition of the body represents the termination of being.

I quote these passages because they illustrate the engagements of people's minds, which the stones they left on our hillsides in the process of dealing with their emotions do not do so clearly. It is of interest to us when confronting the heaped up, jumbled bones within the cromlechs to realise that (at any rate for Gilgamesh) as long as the deceased bear a resemblance to the person's living form they are the subject of individual mourning, and when it is no longer possible to associate the corpse with the person such individual reverence has to stop.

Glyn Daniel quotes an imaginative speculation by Professor Mylonas about the tombs at Mycenae:

> ... burial succeeded burial until the floor-space was occupied and the bodies were decomposed. Then room was made for the latest addition by packing the bones of the ancestors in cists, by sweeping them up against the sides of the grave, or even by throwing them out into the dromos.

Mylonas interprets this as meaning that as long as the flesh was in existence the body had to be treated with respect, but with decomposition, the spirit had left it.

Daniel warns against generalising from this comparison, and it should be recognised that in the various examples concerned here, several not always compatible things are going on. Actual burial in the ground – interment – which is our own recent habit, seems to be rare in prehistory. Indeed, in places where burial in the earth is still impracticable, such as in the high-water-table areas of the Mississippi delta, 'burial' above ground-level is still practised.

Entombment or incineration are the other two remaining choices for disposal of the dead, but as in the case of Gilgamesh who appears to have done neither with Enkidu, the alternative of simple exposure was also always available. In the Zoroastrian religion, practised in Iran since about 1,500 BC, the dead are exposed in burial grounds on structures known as dokhma, which translates as 'Towers of Silence'. An explanation for exposure is that because the body is impure it would defile the sacredness of earth, water or fire. The bones, bleached by the sun, are eventually stored in a pit below the tower. Strangely enough, much the same habit was practised by the Mandan Indians in Upper Missouri, when George Catlin wrote about them in the 1830's, shortly before they were wiped out by a smallpox epidemic. The Mandans exposed their dead on platforms in an area outside the village, later arranging the bleached skulls in circles.

Differences in the treatment of the dead may well reflect differences in ideas about what becomes of them. Belief that the dead are on a journey somewhere (as Homer believed, to Hades), impels the survivors to provide them with sustenance for the journey; a further literal extension of that idea sees them residing in a form modelled on this earthly one, and so the dead provided them with things they would like to have with them on arrival. Elaborate grave-goods appear in Sumerian burials in the third millennium BC in Iraq, and underlining their purpose of accompanying the dead they include sacrificed attendants and guards.

Certain correlations seem obvious. A richer society gives rise to richer burials. Thus in Egypt (where a lot is known about burial habits, partly because of the preservative quality of the dry air) when cultivation first started in the late stone age, the dead were buried in simple pits although even then, before 3,000 BC, with some ordinary personal possession. Elaboration of this fashion came with economic development. Perhaps it was the state of preservation of the ancient dead due to the desert conditions that gave rise to the strong belief in an afterlife, and the increasing concern with means of preservation by mummification. Yet it is impossible, even here, to generalise. In the second oldest class of discovered burials in Egypt, the corpses appear to have been deliberately stripped of flesh, and (as Sir Wallis Budge puts it, in *Egyptian Religion*) 'all the bones are found cast indiscriminately in the grave', sometimes (oddly) the hands and feet bones together, 'while the rest of the skeleton is scattered about in wild confusion'. Yet even in these circumstances the accompanying grave goods, consisting of tools and ornaments, indicate a belief that the deceased was to live a future bodily life.

It is worth acknowledging the widespread habit of sacrificing human beings at the burial of important people, since there are those who believe that the large quantity of bones found in the cromlechs in Wales is evidence of such a

Bryn Celli Ddu.

Maes Howe, Orkneys.

Barclodiad y Gawres

Cromlech Plas Newydd

Cromlech Bodowyr   *Bryn yr Hen Bobol*

Trefignath

Cromlech Pant y Saer

Cromlech Tŷ Newydd, Llanfaelog

37

Cromlech Llugwy

The remains of Cromlech Hen Drefor, Llansadwrn

The cromlechs at Dyffryn Ardudwy

Carneddau Hengwm

Cromlech Corsygedol

Gwerneinion

Cromlech Penarth, Aberdesach

Cromlech Bach Wen, Clynnog Fawr

Cromlech Mynydd Cefnamwlch

Cromlech Abererch

Cromlech Rhos-lan

*The cairn at the summit of
Mynydd Carnguwch*

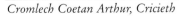

Cromlech Coetan Arthur, Cricieth

Tan y muriau

43

Cromlech Ystum Cegid Isaf

Cromlech Allor Moloch

Llety'r Filiast, Great Orme.

Cromlech Maen y Bardd

Cromlech Capel Garmon

46

*Barclodiad y Gawres,
Bwlch y Ddeufaen*

Cairn on the Gogarth above Llandudno.

Gop

Maen Pebyll

habit. The ancient Maya style of burial, which was uncannily similar to the Egyptian, and which constituted rising levels of pyramid-mounds enclosing the tomb of a ruler, involved the sacrifices of adults and children. Often two or more adolescents accompanied a warrior, and other articles include food, and utensils for its preparation. The approaches to the burial itself were in some cases intentionally blocked, as were those of some of the Welsh cromlechs. In *The Maya*, Michael D. Coe describes one tomb at Palenque as 'a funerary monument with exactly the same primary function as the Egyptian pyramids'.

The Vikings were also well-known also for their display of the evidence of certain tenets of belief regarding the dead, though at a later period. In one magnificent ship-burial, discovered in a mound at Gokstad on the west side of Oslo fjord in 1880, a large boat of the ninth century AD was accompanied by the remains of twelve horses and six dogs. Other goods had already been looted. The Saxon ship-burial at Sutton Hoo near Woodbridge in Suffolk, was found complete in 1939, and contained a considerable amount of jewellery, a shield, a bronze helmet and gold coins.

We are lucky to have a complete description of a tenth-century Viking cremation ceremony, which suggest strongly that the rites were those which had been practised since antiquity. Translated from Arabic, it survived into the present by a complex route, but was published in *Antiquity* in March, 1934. The original author was sent by the Caliph of Baghdad in the year 921 to visit a community of Scandinavians on the Volga. He happened to arrive at the time of the funeral of a great chief. A servant girl volunteered to die with her master. The body was placed with much ceremony in a boat, on top of the funeral pyre, accompanied by a dog, weapons, oxen and cows. After the cremation a mound was raised over the ashes.

One conclusion to draw is that a pattern of actions which is relatively constant from Homer to the tenth century Volga, from Mexico to Egypt, must have something to tell us about the background to the tombs and cairns under consideration here. However, there are variations within the pattern. While the Volga Vikings set fire to the whole lot, covering the residue with a mound in exactly the Homeric fashion, Vikings elsewhere constructed mounds over the body, boat, grave-goods and sacrifices intact. In Britain, when the stage was reached of individual burial, the remains, which were cremated elsewhere, were placed within a structure over which the mound was built. The lack of individual emphasis on the non-cremated bones within the cromlechs argues against the idea of accompanying human sacrifice, and in fact suggests something not dealt with in the literature, namely the concept of *general* rather than *personal* memorial.

THREE
ORIGINS AND DIFFUSION

They were our first farmers. Early Stone Age man hunted and gathered, the small population of the time enabling an easy balance with the sources of supply. Something set off the quest for improvement which put an end to this state of presumed respect and harmony.

There are a number of reasons for viewing the advent of farming as a fall from grace, a loss of innocence, leading to the expulsion from the spiritual garden of Eden. Indeed the Book of Genesis explicitly encourages us to regard it as such: 'Therefore the Lord God sent him forth from the garden of Eden, to till the ground from whence he was taken.'

Farming required a fixed settlement pattern: people had to be present when in due course the seeds they had sown produced crops. With this fixed settlement pattern went the need for social organisation, to deal with the business of living together, and this produced a number of other factors which have since then continuously complicated our lives. Working out a system for social co-existence gives rise to structures of authority, hierarchy and power; another consequence of settled life is a recognition of kinship and allegiance; a proprietorial attitude towards one's own patch. With agriculture comes a growing sense of the causal sequence from past to future, and this multiplied many times produces a sense of our place in time, and the requirement of facing up to and dealing mentally with our mortality. Ideas of generations, and hence of ancestry develop, and of the long flow of our human pilgrimage through time.

Most of all settled agricultural communities developed (along with their increasing ability to manage, rather than simply garner, the natural world, and with a growing emphasis on co-operation and specialisation) newfound elements of surplus and accumulation of reserves which led in due course to the accumulation of wealth and development of social differentiation.

Hence some could now take time off, at least in the quiet seasons, to think – to speculate, to try to understand, and to concern themselves with other non-functional matters as well, such as the building of burial chambers, a means of expressing to themselves, the world, and posterity the conclusions of those speculations.

The 'fall from grace' hypothesis is further supported by the evidence that as the world becomes increasingly subject to human control it becomes, increasingly conceptually problematic.

The ancestors of the grain varieties we use today, and also of some of our domesticated animals, used to grow wild in the hills north of the Euphrates valley. The first tentative steps towards improving these seem to have taken place in northern Iran about 8,000 BC, and had become well established in the Near East a thousand years later. This process gave rise to the foundation of the first towns. However the secret of efficient farming – that is, the replacement of nutrients by fertilisation – for a long time eluded these people. Loss of fertility of the soil after constant cropping gave rise to the movement of populations, and also to a growing competition for fertile land.

There is a traceable progress of early farming people out of Anatolia and subsequently in two directions. One stream went round the northern Mediterranean coast and emerged in the geographical area under consideration. Another stream, which their pottery identifies as being derived from the same source, went up the Danube valley, and in due course, in about 5,000 BC, reached the Rhine. They were still cave-dwellers. 'Indeed', writes Frances Lynch in *Prehistoric Anglesey*, on which much of this discussion is based, 'their main building activity seems to have been concerned with large and complex tombs for the communal burial of the dead'.

Both those population streams in the end approached our western seaboard. The one moving through central Europe can be traced in Poland, Denmark, and eventually Britain. The other following the Mediterranean coastline moved past Almeria, in Spain, then through Portugal and south-west France and in due course up the coast to Brittany and thence perhaps to Cornwall and Ireland. At the same time they went on north to Holland, northern Germany, Denmark and Sweden. The two groups developed different types of tombs, though this is thought to be the expression of differences in religious ideas rather than an expression of any basic variety in their origins. The first type consisted of grouped individual burials, covered by a single mound, identifiable in Brittany by the mid-fifth millennium BC; the second type more the familiar single chambers for communal burials, which then became dominant in most parts of Europe.

It is important to remember that these people were not simply moving into an empty continent. In the Danube valley they encountered a population already in place. The habit initially in this contact zone was to build small graves near to settlements. In fact the incidence of large stone tombs seems to have occurred at the edges of the new economy, rather than at its heart.

During the nineteenth century, and indeed into the twentieth, the interpretation of this apparent connection between the movement of farming people and the building of large stone tombs was clear and simple. An elaborate form had developed in the Near East, as best exemplified by the magnificent monuments of Egypt and Mycenean Greece. The people brought with them memories of these forms, but their abilities and aspirations as pioneers in harder climates declined and degenerated until all that was left was the distant references to the form on the Anglesey coast and Llŷn hillsides. The 'megalithic missionaries' theory was still being assumed by Professor Gordon Childe in the 1930's.

The only trouble with this most comprehensible and reasonable interpretation of these distant events is that it turns out to be largely wrong. From the 1960's on, radiocarbon dating has demolished the theory of the eastern Mediterranean origins of European tomb-building. To take the example of Ireland, it was for a long time thought that the great burial mounds of the Boyne valley were themselves the pale shadow of something that originated in Egypt and Greece, and in the course of the long Irish tradition of the building of burial chambers the Boyne style deteriorated as the colonists moved west. Newgrange has now been carbon-dated to a calendar year around 3,200 BC, making it older than Stonehenge and Avebury. But this also has the effect of making it older than the Egyptian pyramids, and the earliest tombs at Mycenae have been dated to around 1,510 BC. In *Newgrange, archaeology, art and legend* by Michael J. O'Kelly, the author who led the excavations at Newgrange between 1962 and 1975, writes 'In the past it was held that Newgrange was near the end of a line of devolution which had begun in the tholos tombs of Mycenae, but it is clear now that Newgrange is older by at least a thousand years'. Moreover the same process of dating has destroyed the other long-held view, that the relationship between Newgrange and the simpler tombs of western Ireland was one of decline, and deterioration of style. Now, says O'Kelly, '... if an evolutionary sequence is present at all, it must be from the simple to the complex'.

This is something of a revolution. It leaves us with the puzzle as to what exactly was the connection, if any, between farming and tomb-building. Taking the Irish example as a paradigm, it is not difficult to accept the idea of an evolution from simple to elaborate, from **Maen y Bardd** to **Bryn Celli Ddu**, but the idea that the flow of development was also from west to east is problematic. It is scarcely credible that while the farming communities went one way, westwards, their ideas about tomb-building, developing as they went, travelled the other way. Yet the alternative is hardly more probable, even if as Frances Lynch argues, radiocarbon dating has 'shown the phenomenon of monumental burial to be developing in many parts of Europe at about the same time and springing from essentially local reactions to new economies and ways of thinking'.

Of course the fact that the corbelling of the beehive tombs of Mycenae is reminiscent of the corbelling of the main chamber at Newgrange, and that other features of the Boyne tombs recur in Anglesey at Barclodiad y Gawres and Bryn Celli Ddu, is not in itself a compelling reason for supposing an influence flowing between them (whichever way): they could well represent solutions to a common problem – how to roof a tomb. It is rather the idea of the tomb itself, and the similarities of function, which leaves little alternative to the conclusion that there is some connection. Moreover the early graves found by Schliemann at Mycenae included shaft graves similar in form to the Welsh passage graves: two rows of vertical slabs roofed by larger horizontal ones.

It was not always assumed that the movement of ideas came from east to west. During the 1860's and 70's the official theories held that the movement had been from north to south, from the Baltic to Africa. In 1872 James Ferguson proposed in *Rude Stone Monuments in all Countries* the idea of considering the tombs as a consistent style group, rather as one might think of 'Gothic' or 'Grecian', as opposed to the product of migrating people: it was the custom of building them that was diffused, not the builders. This is an approach not dissimilar to actual current thinking, yet it was itself reversed again in the twentieth century, when theoretical explanations returned to the idea of migrations. Glyn Daniel, who outlines this theoretical background in *The Megalith Builders of Western Europe*, calls this approach 'monocentric hyper-diffusion', and comments that 'there are not many who today regard the megalithic monuments of the world as remains of wandering Egyptians'.

'Are the megalithic monuments of the world the result of the spread of people (or influences) from one centre, or are they not?' he asks. At least in the eyes of modern experts in the field, such as Frances Lynch, the answer, now, is no. In the 1950's Daniel was already prepared to accept this. 'Others have argued,' he writes, 'that there is very little in common between the structures in different parts of the world designated as megaliths, save the use of large stones, and that this use of large stones might well have arisen independently in different parts of the world'. This contradicts the position he more conventionally took up when he argued that 'all the evidence now available suggests that the chamber tombs were diffused to the British Isles by a folk movement of colonists ...'

Whatever the general position world-wide, it is recognised that the tombs in Wales show signs of influence from elsewhere. The Anglesey group, for instance, appears to have roots in the passage-grave cultures of western Europe: Iberia, Brittany, and Ireland. There are other reasons for concluding that Anglesey has frequently, in early times, been more or less an Irish colony. There is no denying the similarity of form, though not of size, between **Barclodiad y Gawres** and **Bryn Celli Ddu** on the one hand, and Newgrange and its neighbours on the other, so that although of course it could conceivably have been the other way round, Daniel is perhaps right to say that at least some of this was 'probably a colonial extension of the Boyne culture'.

FOUR
A CLOSER LOOK

Anglesey/Ynys Môn

Frances Lynch identifies Neolithic tombs on Anglesey. The map in the Royal Commission on Ancient Monuments Inventory shows twenty-eight. Since not all those that are now identifiable have stood the test of time all that well, some being now no more than heaps of stones, it is a certainty that there must once have been many more, all punctuating the surface of Anglesey at the same time. This indicates the density of the population of Neolithic Anglesey, but also tells us something about the use of the tombs: each social group – extended families, or 'kindred groups' – felt the need to have each their own tomb, rather than share them with neighbours.

In location the tombs cluster recognisably, seeking the coastal belts of fertile land. The central area, which was (and still partly is) marshy and hard to farm, was entirely avoided. The western and southern stretches of the coast, better sheltered, were favoured then, as indeed they are today, as places of settlement.

One thing that strikes one at once is the great diversity in form and size which these, the remaining examples, display. Since there are such good specimens of these still standing I shall concentrate here on the best of them, and not spend time discussing and describing the rather sad remains of those which have declined from their once proud prominence to resembling the natural outcrops out of which they were, in the first place, presumably drawn.

It should be remembered (though it continues to be surprising) that the form in which they were intended to be seen was not these magnificent stone structures, but that of large mounds, or small hills.

That being the case it is natural to start with those that are in this form at present: the two most famous of Anglesey's tombs, **Bryn Celli Ddu** and **Barclodiad y Gawres**. It must be said that the form in which they are now to be seen is the result of restoration, and for that reason they lack the atmosphere of some of the other more gaunt remains. Old drawings show **Bryn Celli Ddu** bare, but when first recorded it had been covered as it is now, since the first explorers of it crept along its passage with lanterns. It was excavated and restored to its present form between 1927 and 1931 by W. J. Hemp, Inspector of Ancient Monuments for Wales, who revealed its unusual feature, an apparent bench of flat stones set into the clay of the north wall of the passage. Hemp noted the only human remains then, fragments of cremated bone 'deliberately scattered' on the floor, together with some bits of unburnt bone. Skeletons had been removed from the tomb before his time. Originally the passage had been completely blocked with stones and earth. Discovery of white quartz pebbles all over the site links this form with the burial mounds of the Boyne valley, and rather suggests that the mound itself was designed to be a striking visible feature, and not to be grassed over as it is at present. Besides the central pillar by which **Bryn Celli Ddu** is distinguished, a stone was found lying flat on the floor – and its position made it clear that this was intended – which had an incised pattern on each side. It has been suggested concluded that this must have been upright during some ceremony, and after that would have been laid flat.

Hemp viewed the monument as being of one period, but

it is now known to reflect two distinct phases. Frances Lynch even considers these to represent two different religions, one long-established, one more recently introduced. The first phase was a ditch and circle of stones. The passage grave, when built, overlay this earlier feature and obscured it. It is thought this latter structure was one of the last of its kind, since the henge form over which it is built was itself not older than the middle Neolithic period.

Barclodiad y Gawres, near Aberffraw, is on a sea-blown pitching headland, and again, until its restoration, was visible as only a sprawl of massive stones. The name, however, indicates that it must in early times have presented the form of a large pile of regular stones, not, as at present, a grassy hill: it means 'the giantess's apronful'. The name occurs elsewhere in connection with a story of a giant and giantess carrying stones to build a house, she containing them in her apron. These two will appear again, next time in connection with a Bronze Age cairn.

Barclodiad y Gawres was thoroughly excavated in 1952-3, and unfortunately it was rebuilt, so that you cannot now see what it was originally like. The dig revealed, however, a number of remarkable and distinctive features. One was that its cruciform shape indicated its relationship to the Boyne culture of Ireland. Another (which also indicated this relationship) was its five decorated stones. Some of these indeed bear the serial double-spirals so strongly associated with Newgrange. The only other example of this art form in Wales, as far as I know, is the single stone now in the church at Llanbedr, near Harlech, which itself was probably brought from a now-lost burial chamber. A pattern remarkably similar to the ones here may be seen on some slabs known as the Calderstones, which once formed part of a chamber tomb near Liverpool, and which are now in the City of Liverpool museum.

Something quite remarkable at **Barclodiad y Gawres** was what appeared to be the remains of a ritual meal. Fortunately this had been apparently deliberately preserved by packing seashells over it. A fire had been lit on the floor of the central chamber, and this had been dowsed with a remarkable stew containing, among other things, eel, frog, toad, grass snake, mouse, and shrew. It was therefore probably never intended for consumption. What the ritual function of this extraordinary procedure was is likely to remain, one feels, beyond speculation.

What these and the other tombs looked like over much of their history can be seen from one tomb which has simply kept its mound intact. This is **Bryn yr Hen Bobl**, which lies on private land at Plas Newydd, but is fully described in Frances Lynch's Prehistoric Anglesey. The mound is still eighteen foot high, giving the appearance of a small hill, as the name suggests: the hill of the old people. This name itself is of interest, since it indicates a disjunction in Anglesey's occupation: the people who gave the hill its name were perhaps aware of there having been a previous and distinct population.

Bryn yr Hen Bobl was excavated in 1929-35 by W. J. Hemp. Inhumations were discovered in the form of unburnt bones that were much damaged and mixed together, possibly the result of later disturbance. Later burials on top of the cairn had become mixed up with them, so that the original number of people buried could not be ascertained. Nevertheless, the remains of about twenty people were accounted for, of mixed ages, including an infant under a year old.

One strange feature of **Bryn yr Hen Bobl** is an area to the south of the cairn known as the 'terrace', a long thin stone-built platform, 330 feet long and 40 feet wide, surrounded by a two-foot high wall. This evidently contrived to be of sacred significance, since a Bronze Age urn burial was found at the south end.

Under this platform, on the old ground surface, Neolithic pottery, stone axes and flints were found. A settlement had evidently existed here before the tomb was built, possibly of Middle Stone Age date (as recent studies of the flints have suggested). Some of the pottery was related in style to examples from southern England, indicating contact, or perhaps even immigration. The cairn has a well-defined entrance, and in the forecourt of this were found signs of four separate fires, perhaps indicating four different ceremonial occasions.

Not far away, on the lawn stretching down towards **Plas Newydd** itself, a magnificent double-chambered structure reclines on the slope. The form is unusual, possibly unlike any other, since the large northern chamber is blocked off from the smaller one by a supporting stone to the northern capstone, so that the two chambers are not linked, and it is probably misleading therefore to refer to the smaller chamber (as the Royal Commission on Ancient Monuments Inventory does) as an antechamber or passage.

Several of the Anglesey tombs have been thoroughly investigated, some in modern times, and they reveal much about the function and original form of the others. One such tomb is the large denuded gallery grave **Trefignath**, near Holyhead. This is an illustration of the striking characteristic of Anglesey tombs: they are often quite unlike each other. **Trefignath** is described by W. F. Grimes as a segmented cist, by others as a gallery or passage grave, but is probably best known now as a long cairn or chambered tomb. It consists of a vast sprawl of stones surrounding two visible chambers, unconnected, rather like the ones of the monument at **Plas Newydd**, one of the chambers having a pair of uprights appearing to form an entrance (rather than supporting the capstone). It is built on the natural base of a solid outcrop of limestone forming an elevated platform, which contributes to its visual impact.

The lack of access between the two (originally three) chambers is significant, since it distinguishes this tomb from the Irish examples of gallery graves. Excavations carried on towards the end of the 1970's, occasioned by the collapse of the central chamber in 1979, showed quite clearly that the three separate chambers were built in succession from west to east over probably quite a long period, in different styles derived presumably from different influences, and that the last one, which is of quite a different nature, with its two tall portal stones, blocked off the central one. The length of the gap between the building of the chambers is not known, but increase in pollen from grasses and arable plants, as opposed to trees, in samples found below the first and second phases of cairn-building, indicates improvement in farming and perhaps some clearance in between. Finds on the site show it to have been used for a considerable period, starting with a time of domestic use in about 3,000 BC, before the first cairn was built, so that interestingly it appears that the burial took place on inhabited land. The first chamber is considered to be of the Simple Passage Grave type, while the last chamber approaches (but does not quite conform to) the 'Portal Dolmen' form. Excavation showed that the cairn was expanded and adapted to incorporate the successive phases of chamber construction. In the Monograph reporting the dig, the excavators Dr. C. A. Smith and Frances Lynch conclude about Trefignath (and elsewhere) that 'the composite tomb has now been recognised as so widespread a class of monument that there must be some doubt about the contemporaneous development of all but the most unitary structures'. This is, and is intended to be, a radical revision of the previous supposition that these monuments were built in a single period.

A second and similar site was excavated starting in the late 60's and only finally concluded in 1980. This was the much less well-preserved tomb between Llangefni and Aberffraw known as **Din Dryfol.** Also classified as a Passage Grave, **Din Dryfol** was found to date from the same period – that is about 3,000 BC. Also composite and developed over several stages, its main feature is the remains of a rectangular chamber, flanked by portal stones, one of which remains prominently in place. The second chamber, which is not so evident now, was found to have had wooden entrance posts, which was considered unusual – though these might of course have existed undetected elsewhere. Unlike those at **Trefignath**, which are aligned to the chamber, the portal stones here are set at right angles to the chamber, and the passage between the chambers appears to have been unobstructed. Not far from the tomb is a large unexcavated barrow.

Although it is suspected that many or most of these monuments were of composite form, built in stages over a long time-span, and went through successive periods of use like these two, there are some on Anglesey that appear to have been simple single chambers. The distinction is perhaps not as clear as it looks, since some of these, such as **Bodowyr,** near the farm of that name north-west of Bryn Siencyn, which now appear to be classic examples of a single chamber, were originally entered by a passage, and hence might qualify as a Passage Grave. All of course, were covered by a mound and so had at least an element of cairn about them.

Bodowyr, though modest by some standards, is the perfect specimen of a cromlech, though it loses some element of mystery by being surrounded by neat Cadw railings. Its eight-foot-long capstone perches provocatively on three uprights, as with many other such monuments challenging the modern observer to guess how it got there, and here it is harder than ever to remember that those who built it did not intend that it should ever be seen.

One tomb in Anglesey which is important more for the revelation of its excavation than for its innate interest is Pant y Saer, near Benllech. It consists of a monumental fallen capstone leaning on the shoulders of two uprights. In its raised clearing in a natural setting, still primevally among gorse and thorn, it has the benefit of that fine Anglesey view of the whole stretch of the Snowdonia mountain. It is best reached from the Llangefni road out of Benllech, where a footpath to it is signposted.

Pant y Saer was excavated by Lindsay Scott in 1930 and 1932, and bones from the remains of more than fifty people were found within its chamber. The exact number of people varies according to which bones are counted, as these were randomly jumbled and do not constitute complete skeletons. Some skulls and long bones, for instance, were missing, suggesting their use in rituals elsewhere. The point of special interest about these finds, and the thing which makes **Pant y Saer** of importance, is that fifty bodies would not fit into this rather small chamber if they were, at the time, whole. This proves that the tomb was a receptacle for bones rather than persons, and that presumably as new interments had to be added the previous remains were pushed aside. This also indicates that the tomb was in use over a long period, which is consistent with evidence from those elsewhere. Some of the deaths appear to have been in the course of child-birth, since nine full-term foetuses were among the remains.

Another tomb featuring a double chamber, once again apparently not in connected form, is **Presaddfed**, near Bodedern. Here one chamber, with a fine long capstone, is still standing, while the other has fallen, and has only one stone still upright. Like so many of these monuments this one proclaims such confidence that it is amazing to think it was intended to be hidden by a mound.

There is some reason to think (from old accounts) that the single chamber at **Tŷ Newydd**, near Llanfaelog, which is now a huge capstone supported by brick pillars, but was clearly originally resting on top of relatively slender upright stones, was once part of a double-chambered complex. Assuming that the second chamber was needed because the first was full indicates use by a large population over a considerable time. When one considers how many people it would take to raise even this single remaining capstone, the evidence seems to conflict with the idea of these tombs being used by a single kinship group. **Tŷ Newydd** was excavated in 1935, and the excavation revealed the rather surprising result that it was floored with a covering of black earth containing large quantities of charcoal, among which were also a large number of white quartz chippings. Today screaming jets from Valley criss-cross the overhead sky.

Another amazingly bulky capstone is that of the chamber at **Llugwy**, near Moelfre, an area perhaps better known for its Iron Age village. The effect of the mass is rather lessened by the unusual shortness of the uprights, so that it squats like a giant beetle, almost on the ground. This visual effect is because (as is the case at **Pant y Saer**) the chamber makes use of a pit, so that what is seen above ground is only a third of the chamber's full height. When the tomb was excavated by Neil Baynes in 1908, fragmentary remains of about thirty people were found in a burial area in two layers divided by paving. The upper layer, interestingly, was covered by limpet shells. Along with the human bones (unburnt, mixed and broken) a wide variety of animal bones were also found.

All of the foregoing are only the most revealing sample of the Anglesey chambers, and ruined and in some cases neglected examples also abound – at **Hen Drefor** near Pentraeth, for example; at **Llanfechell**, now no more than a heap of stones; at **Perthiduon**, Llanidan, and doubtless at many other sites.

There is no clear distinction between the cairns that cover group burial chambers, such as **Bryn yr Hen Bobl**, and the cairns that cover single burials, but the Anglesey examples of the later, Bronze Age tombs offer us a possible subdivision of these: there are those, such as the cairns on **Holyhead Mountain** and the two cairns on the rocky ridge known as **Garn**, which are overtly prominent, and there are the many low and inconspicuous barrows, scarcely more than a hump in a field. The cairn on the summit of Holyhead mountain itself is now largely dispersed, though the base of it may still be seen. Other summit cairns in

Anglesey may be found on **Mynydd Bodafon** and **Mynydd Llwydiarth**. It is perhaps the distribution of the identifiable barrows which is of the greatest interest in this transition from the Stone Age to the Bronze.

During this period there is no noticeable clustering, as was the case earlier, which was then around the fertile and sheltered areas of the Menai Strait and the eastern coast. Instead there is a fairly even spread throughout the island, though the boggy centre is still avoided. Now the previously neglected north end is also evidently in use, a sign, it is thought, of the combination of drier conditions and increased population.

In the cases where finds have been made at these barrows it is not always possible to determine which are primary and which have been added to the barrow after it was built. In the case of the mound at **Tre Iorwerth**, near the double cromlech **Presaddfed**, at Bodedern, some burials seem to have been added as late as Roman, or even early Christian times. This burial site has points in common with **Bedd Branwen**, one more recently investigated and not far away.

Bedd Branwen, on the river Alaw at Llanbabo, would be of interest if only for its name, which connects it with the Mabinogi story of Branwen, daughter of Llŷr. It is a sad tale of some complexity, concerning the unhappy marriage of Branwen, the sister of Brân, king of Britain, to the king of Ireland, which resulted in war between the two countries. Branwen, returning to Anglesey, looking back at Ireland, is overcome with remorse for the wars and the loss of life which she has caused. 'And she heaved a great sigh, and with that broke her heart. And a four-sided grave was made for her, and she was buried there on the bank of the Alaw.'

The spot has traditionally been known as Branwen's island, but it was not until 1813 that a tumulus was found there containing an urn with the cremated remains of a simple Bronze Age burial. A handful of scattered stones is visible there now, near the small and wandering Alaw. The site was fully excavated in 1967 by Frances Lynch, and it was found that the barrow had been erected around a central standing stone, which itself dated to before 1,400 BC. A low mound of earth originally surrounded the central stone, which it is thought would have remained visible.

Many of Anglesey's barrows are, like Bedd Branwen, set inconspicuously on undistinguished sites, but one which is exceptional for its prominence, being most unusually on a slope and rising some six foot high, is the one known simply as **Garn**, quite near Bryn Siencyn.

Ardudwy

That Anglesey has no Portal Dolmens, and that this form is so characteristic of the Harlech area, indicates a rather unexpected distinction in Stone Age population. The conclusion that a settled population with established habits was in place in Anglesey when the builders of the other style arrived is not borne out by the relative dating, since the Anglesey tombs are thought on the whole to be later than those along Cardigan Bay; moreover several of them show influence of the Portal form, but without the high, prominent portal itself. The style is so distinctive that it looks as if the capstones of the chambers along the Harlech coast are just about to slide off. An introductory example is the tomb at **Gwern Einion**, up a lane in the hinterland between Llanfair and Llanbedr. Though it is now built into a farm wall and put to use as a shelter for animals, this is an extreme example of the tilted capstone which results directly from the high raised portals. Here you can also see the other main characteristic, the closing stone across the 'portal' itself, which gives to this style of building the form often referred to as an H. Anglesey chambers, by contrast, mainly have their capstones set at a firm and magnificent horizontal, and lack also the mysterious blocking stone across their entrances. This is mysterious because at least in some cases the blocking stone can be shown to be a part of the original construction, not a final addition. As Glyn Daniel points out, the vast majority of tombs in England and Wales were open, as a result of which they could be serially re-used. Some, however, were closed when they were constructed, indicating that they could only have been used once. **Dyffryn Ardudwy** illustrates this point.

Here, just behind the school, is a double-chambered complex united by a single mound, a general form. This was excavated in the 1960's, and shown then to have been of more than one period of construction. The lower, western chamber is the older, and represents a classic example of this type of tomb. The upper one, in any case of a much less pure form, has been rather unpleasantly reinforced.

It is the lower chamber that is of interest here. When built, it had its own cairn, the remains of which can be seen around its feet. This, and the walled forecourt at the (supposed) entrance to the tomb, was covered by the extended cairn which then linked it with the later tomb when that was built. Once again the whole then remained a place of veneration for some time, as is clear from the placing within it of a Bronze Age cremation.

The blocking stone of the lower chamber is squeezed between the two portal stones, which appear to be leaning on it, perhaps even supported by it. Its position is such (interior to the portal stones) that it could not have been put in place *after* they were erected. It is therefore, in its present and original position, a part of the original constructional design of the chamber. Yet this stone does not support the roof, nor does it completely block the place which, by its two prominent door-pillars and the forecourt leading to it, was clearly intended to be seen as the entrance. You can see in over it; the one thing you cannot do, because of its position, is enter the tomb.

Frances Lynch is of the opinion that bones, perhaps even bodies, could be passed into the tomb over the top of the blocking stone. That is certainly the case here, and perhaps is possible in general with blocked tombs. But since many tombs are easily re-entered, and there is evidence of long and repeated use, *why* is it felt necessary in some cases to make it impossible to get in? Clearly a belief of some sort was held here which subsequently ceased to be subscribed to elsewhere, or which had not yet, in other cases, come into being. It is also possible that something which appears to be for the purpose of preventing the living from getting in, might in fact have been intended to prevent the dead getting out.

Of a a rather different form are the two sets of cairns and chambers known as **Carneddau Hengwm**, further south, near Tal y Bont. Impressive for their size and setting, these badly-damaged monuments are of interest as being of a type associated with south Wales, and linked in style to the Cotswold-Severn type of tomb. The remains of a portal here also associate the eastern chamber with those that have already been discussed, and an unusual feature is a chamber constructed of dry-stone walling, still with its capstone present, the chamber of which is entered by a passage from the side. The combination of styles seems to indicate a conjunction of influences taking place here, perhaps over a succession of periods.

At **Cors y Gedol**, also near Tal y Bont, the capstone fell long ago, but it seems that a rectangular chamber once formed the focus of a long barrow running for about 90 feet east to west. As in all these cases, the cairn was evidently of a distinctly elongated shape.

The coincidence of styles at this point, styles that link these monuments both to Ireland and to southern Britain, particularly the Cotswold area, suggests the arrival of influences via trade routes, this being a natural stopping point on the route between those two areas of intense Neolithic activity. The river Artro, offering a haven at its mouth near Llandanwg, may be seen as a factor in this.

A glance at the map provided by W. F. Grimes in *The Megalithic Monuments of Wales* reveals something else about the Ardudwy tombs which is of more general interest. Thickly clustered around the coasts of Anglesey and Llŷn, their spread continues down this coast, no less than seven of them then occurring in Ardudwy. They then stop, quite suddenly, at this point near Tal y Bont. The coast continues with no sign of a change in character, but the tombs do not re-occur until Pembrokeshire – to be precise, in the Nevern and Newport area, at the seaward foot of the Preseli hills. Here there is a great mass of them, including the magnificently long-capstoned **Pentre Ifan**.

To seaward of Llanaber lies the lost kingdom of Cantre Gwaelod. The 'bottom hundred' was a rich and fertile land, but it was low-lying and in danger from the sea. Flood-gates protected it from the incoming tide, and were left open to drain it on the ebb. One night the drunken keeper of the gates forgot to close them. The idyllic kingdom went under the sea.

This is supposed to have happened during the sixth century, the time in Wales of small kingdoms. Carbon dating of tree-roots elsewhere along the coast has given a much earlier date for the flourishing of now drowned lands: some seven thousand years ago. The distribution of these tombs gives a past cut-off point: on the reasoning that the tombs do not continue down the present coastline because it was not then the coastline, its original line was obliterated not earlier than a time between 2000 and 3,000 BC.

Llŷn/Eifionydd

There are two tombs worth visiting on the approach to the Llŷn peninsula from the Caernarfon direction. One, known as **Penarth**, lies up a lane opposite Aberdesach, and is now in a state of magnificent collapse, resembling a giant mushroom. Its packing stones can be seen under the fallen capstone, and a clear ring of stones runs around it.

Down at Clynnog Fawr itself, below the church and very close to the sea, the cromlech at **Bach Wen** is reached down a long green lane bordered with beach-stone walls, and is itself set on a slope above the sea, with views to Dinas Dinlle and Tre'r Ceiri on Yr Eifl. The stones which once formed the cairn over this tomb may perhaps be seen now in the fine stone walls bordering the fields around it. This chamber is unusual for the so-called cupmarks on the top of the capstone, which are still visible if you know they are there, but are now indistinct. There are said to be 110 of these on the upper surface alone, and a few more on the sides. It is considered possible by some that these were a later addition, but nobody knows what they may have at any time signified.

Taking the coast road through Tudweiliog, the small but elegant cromlech on **Mynydd Cefn Amwlch** is to be found below the wood, just above the Sarn Meyllteyrn road which forks off the coast road. It is notable for the prominent ridge on top of its capstone, which rests confidently on three uprights to form a perfect roof. What is particularly interesting in this example is the even flattening of the underside, which seems unlikely to have occurred naturally, and so indicates that this effect was intended to be seen, from within the chamber, presumably, since the signs of a barrow around are a reminder that the fine ridge on top would not have been visible.

Harder to find, and on private land (though permission to view is readily given) is the large complex monument at **Tan y Muriau**, on Mynydd Rhiw. It lies behind the house, up the hill, and is partly obscured by later walling, by vegetation and, in the summer, is covered in bracken. It is most notable for its vast eleven foot wide, thirteen foot long capstone, resting now at a severe tilt on a lower upright, which has evidently sunk. Inside the chamber, seen from underneath the capstone, the entrance of a Portal Dolmen with its characteristic closing stone classifies at least this part of the monument. As a whole it is of the long cairn form, with two chambers (originally apparently three) probably from different periods, linked by their stone mound. What makes this example unusual is the sheer size and weight of its capstone.

At **Abererch**, south of Y Ffôr, where the farm is called Cromlech after its monument, a fine chamber in an outstanding position with a far outlook across Cardigan Bay had fallen and become ruined by 1869. It collapsed further later that century, but was reconstructed in 1936. It seems from early accounts that this was originally part of a larger ritual complex, since an avenue of stones is referred to which can no longer be discerned.

Moving towards Cricieth, a fine example of the level-capstone type stands in a field near **Rhos-lan**, again, like the **Cefnamwlch** chamber, presenting the surprise of its levelled underside, contrasting with its rounded top. This massive capstone rests precariously on a long back slab and two side pillars, with a gaping open front on the south side where a stone appears to be missing.

Just further east of the tomb at Rhos-lan is the unusual flat-topped chamber of Ystum Cegid Isaf, notable for the thinness of its long capstone. Forming part of a field boundary now, it consists of five uprights supporting the remarkably flat, wedge-shaped top. Possibly originally a passage grave – Pennant, in the eighteenth century, saw three chambers here – it appears from records to have fallen into ruin in the nineteenth century, and so must be, in its present form, rebuilt.

Somewhat inaccessible on the lower slopes of Moel y Gest, west of Porthmadog and north of Morfa Bychan, **Cist Cerrig** consists now of what appears to be the portal part of a Portal Dolmen. Nearby are to be found faint cupmarks like those at **Bach Wen**, but this time on a rock face, not on the tomb itself. 'Cist' (pronounced with a hard 'c') is the Welsh for chest, in the sense of container, itself derived from the Latin *Cista*, a chest or casket. The word has entered the language of archaeology, and now describes the burial chamber within a Bronze Age cairn. In English it is normally mispronounced 'sist'.

Of these cairns, there are several fine examples on Llŷn. One of the most visited is the cairn that preceded the Iron Age hillfort, Tre'r Ceiri, on the summit of **Yr Eifl**. This should perhaps not be taken to indicate continuous use of this site over thousands of years, since a place of such prominence is suited to two different uses – that of memorial, and that of defence. This was a large cairn, some 45 foot across, the top of which has now been levelled to form the site of a modern one.

From there may be seen the sites of other cairns. The one on **Carn Fadrun** also shares its location with an Iron Age fort, and in this case the relation is accidentally closer, since it has been robbed of its stones presumably to build the later, though still ancient, ramparts. What is left shows that the centre of it consisted of a rectangular cist, eight foot by four, formed out of large slabs set on edge.

The most notable of the Llŷn cairns is that on **Mynydd Carnguwch**, which towers above you as you approach the thousand-foot summit. It is about twenty feet high, but inspection reveals that this impression of apparent size is largely due to the particular use of the site: it clothes the conical summit of the mountain. As the primary burial, which was probably in a central pit that appears to have been re-opened, was actually on the ground surface of the hill's summit, the piling up of this enormous heap evidently had a purely monumental function. Pennant, visiting in the eighteenth century, thought it was the remains of a tower. He spotted 'certain facings of a central cell still remaining', and indeed the structure seems to have been founded by revetment, over which it has (intentionally or accidentally) spread.

Mynydd Rhiw was evidently an area of much early activity, since along with the cromlech already mentioned there is the site of a stone axe factory, and no less than two, possibly originally three, Bronze Age cairns. One of these is about 45 feet wide and ten foot high, but the other is now ruined and obscured by later works.

Dyffryn Conwy and Great Orme

Above the Conwy valley are a number of chamber tombs which bear two strikingly distinctive characteristics, both of them in regard to their location: they are away from the sea, and they are high up. One exception to this is the hefty but undistinguished tomb near Hendrewaelod, in Glan Conwy, once known as Allor Moloch, Moloch's Altar, where a capstone estimated to weigh some 22 tons rests now lopsidedly on five uprights. The two tall portal stones flanking its entrance distinguish it from other Conwy valley tombs and relate it to the group that Grimes terms the 'western long cairns'. The location of this one is surprising, being so low in the valley and so close to the river that it must have been built in dense scrub or even forest. Down here in the valley it is not hard to understand the apparently normal tendency of the time to seek out headlands exposed to the constant sea-wind. Another valley-bottom chamber is to be found at **Porth Llwyd**, near Dolgarrog, the exact shape of which has been obscured by damage done to it in the flood resulting from a burst dam in 1925.

At a height of just over 1,000 feet, **Maen y Bardd,** above Ro-wen, is among the highest chambers in Wales, and probably owes its location to the existence of an ancient trackway, which in due course became the Roman road and in later ages (improbable as this now seems) a coaching route. Built on a slope, on the lower edges of Tal y Fan, this small but spectacular monument juts heroically into the sweeping view of the valley below. This, in connection with other such chambers, was once also known by the name of Cwt y Filiast, 'the hut of the greyhound bitch'. The story behind the name concerns a giant, standing in this case on Pen y Gaer (or maybe sitting in his stone armchair which forms the summit of Pen y Gader) whose dog, hunting on these slopes, went to earth in this chamber. He threw his stick at it, which stuck in the ground a little short of the target, and still stands, a narrow, slanting standing stone, behind the wall on the other side of the Roman road on the westerly side. **Maen y Bardd** is the classic example of a single simple chamber, with no sign now of a passage or a mound, though it is thought, because of its shape, to have been originally part of a passage grave. This is an area of intense prehistoric activity, and some fifty yards to the east lies another though lesser chambered barrow.

Like **Maen y Bardd**, the rightly famous chambered long cairn at **Capel Garmon** is also notable for being inland and elevated. **Capel Garmon** consists of three compartments, and so is reminiscent of **Trefignath** near Holyhead, but in fact is unlike **Trefignath** in that here the chambers are joined, forming a single complex evidently designed to function together, whereas in the Anglesey example the three chambers were separate, though contained in one cairn, and so probably belonged to successive periods. At **Capel Garmon** the mound is, unusually, largely intact, and enough of the original packing material of dry-stone walling between the uprights is still in place to show how these structures were originally put together. The entrance passage is at right angles to the alignment of the chambers, and to the south originally deliberately blocked and then evidently hidden by the mound. The present entrance is a later element, this tomb having gone through a long history of adaptation. In the nineteenth century the western chamber was used as a stable. Early clearance meant that when it was finally excavated there were few finds. Some scraps of bone and sherds of Neolithic pottery, and some Bronze Age fragments of the Beaker period testified to its long period of use, or perhaps represented an early instance of re-use.

The mound is wedge-shaped, and in the thicker, eastern end two projecting horns form a forecourt like that of the entrance to some other tombs. Here, white quartz pebbles were found, suggesting perhaps a ritual function of this space. At the back of this indenture in the mound upright slabs indicate a portal, the interesting thing about which is that it is false: there never was a way into the tomb at this point. Why should it have been thought suitable that anyone would be led to suppose that there was? Grimes speculates in the 1950's: 'in conjunction with the entrance-blocking its purpose is to isolate the dead by deceiving dead and living alike as to the ways into and out of the tomb.' This characteristic – the false portal in a forecourt, and the entrance from the side – relates this tomb to the general Cotswold-Severn group, which seems to have found its way up through Wales from the south, via Brecon and Hereford. Grimes, who was then Director of the Institute of Archaeology, states with his characteristic confidence and authority that it was 'the work of people who came to

Britain from western France by way of the Bristol Channel'. Its location here, high up and inland, may be due, he thinks, to arrival of the colonists not by sea but by an overland movement from the Cotswold-Severn areas.

Even higher, up behind Nebo, at a height of 1,100 feet, at the base of moorland rising to the wild, uninhabited land of Hiraethog, where amazing miles of empty country stretch in the Denbigh direction to horizons of distant hills, stands **Maen Pebyll** which offers little to see now, as it seems to have suffered a determined attempt to break it up. It is a pile of large stones, with signs of a broad mound around it, that was presumably cleared some time ago for farming. The name attracts some attention. Pebyll is thought to be a corruption of 'pabell', a tent, but the Nant Conwy Antiquarian Society, which investigated the site in 1909, disagree, claiming that: 'etymologists of note unhesitatingly say it is the Celtic form of Papilius or Popilius, a Roman name, which seems to be most probable'. This is of little help, since it gives not indication who Papilius or Popilius was, nor what Romans were supposed to be doing up here at all, let alone in 3,000 BC. Glyn Daniel, however, claims that it is not a burial chamber anyway, but a long barrow, and the stones here are the components of a menhir, or upright pillar. A drawing of 1850, published by Bezant Lowe, appears to confirm this.

Names and stories tend to recur in connection with these monuments, and the greyhound bitch from the slopes of Tal y Fan, hiding in **Maen y Bardd**, appears again on the Great Orme, where the cromlech at the side of the old mining town, now below the tramway's halfway station, is known as **Llety'r Filiast**, her lodging. The story is presumably similar to the **Maen y Bardd** one.

The Great Orme, closely surrounded by the sea and jutting out defiantly into its climate, treeless due to the porosity of the limestone, is exactly the sort of place one would expect to find signs of early land-use. Indeed at the far western end there are hut circles, which may be Bronze Age but are more likely later, and several chamber tombs were lost during the construction of the Marine Drive, while in 1879 human remains (and numerous animal bones) were found, dating to the Neolithic period, in a cave near Tŷ Gwyn Road, known as Kendrick's Cave.

Llety'r Filiast is a standard, level-roofed construction, with four uprights in place that support a capstone parts of which have broken off and are now lying on the ground. It is described by Daniel as a long barrow, 85 feet by 40, these visible remains constituting its chamber, sited at the south-eastern end. But the axis of the barrow does not seem to conform to the alignment of the chamber, and the mound, which is partly made of natural rock, may in fact be a natural and not a man-made feature, perhaps modified to contribute to the setting of the cromlech.

The Great Orme, is noted for its Bronze Age activity: its world famous copper mines were in operation as early as 1,800 BC and produced in their long history between 10,000 and 50,000 tonnes of copper ore. The Bronze Age cairn at the western end of the headland is about all the visible evidence of the non-mining activities of these people, and according to the Ancient Monuments Inventory this is a case of a modern cairn overlaying an ancient one. Boulders on the north-east side may perhaps be the remains of the kerb of the original.

Denbighshire

It is unusual to find much from the Neolithic period far from the sea, and so **Tyddyn Bleiddyn**, inland from Bodelwyddan, some five miles from the nearest sea near Rhyl is surprising. This is a long barrow with a chamber in one end and originally one other chamber, which was excavated in 1871 but is now lost. This is a badly ruined site, and from the start must have been fairly undistinguished, since it lacks all outlook. It lies well below the treeline in a lush area of native oaks, and so was originally in a clearance in a forest area, so that no idea of a view can have played any part in the choice of location. Now this is rolling wooded fertile farmland, still surrounded by native trees – ash, oak, thorn, hazel, holly.

In terms of outlook a striking contrast is presented by the great mound at **Gop**, rising above Trelawnyd, near Dyserth. In one of the caves below, a stone burial chamber was found in 1886 – the only burial chamber, apparently, in Flintshire. The mound itself, clearly stone-built under its turf, is the largest cairn in Wales, and is said to be the second largest in Europe. It is approached through sweet-scented pine woodland, at the edge of which wide views open inland over mature farmland, of large-squared chequerboard field-patterns, stretching to the far distance towards England, while, to the north, the view reaches to Snowdonia. The other way a long coastal view stretches towards Liverpool. The mound is a huge, steep-sided smooth dome, with a large hollow in its centre. The site was excavated in the 1930's and the finds were sent to London, but were lost in the Blitz.

Gop is of special interest also because of a persistent

legend associated with it. This is said to be the burial place of Bodicca, or less correctly Boadicea. According to the story, below **Gop** is the site of the last battle between the warrior queen and Suetonius Paulinus, Roman governor of Britain. What the queen of the Iceni was supposed to be doing in Wales the story does not explain. However Tacitus is explicit: Suetonius broke off his invasion of Anglesey and marched to Londinium. He decided not to stay and fight there, as he was outnumbered. Instead he let Londinium fall, and the fall of Verulanium followed. Suetonius then gathered further troops and decided to attack the rebels. It is not said where, but it is known that he came from London to carry out the attacks, not, for instance, from northern Wales. The Romans secured a major victory, and the queen, seeing her side losing, poisoned herself rather than surrender. Why this should ever have been thought to be at **Gop** remains a mystery. A rival story, incidentally, puts her burial place below Platform 9, St Pancras Station.

Cairns as burial mounds are so frequent in the more mountainous areas that it may be supposed that this great cairn at **Gop** was originally for that purpose. Along with the isolated example on the Great Orme, which has already been mentioned, the Ancient Monuments Inventory lists more than thirty cairns in the area between Dyffryn Conwy and the north-western coast. Many of them are high in the hills. A group of seven cairns, for instance, representing something reasonably called a cairn cemetery, lies at 900 feet above Aber, and several others occur on the upper slopes of the Anafon valley as it rises towards Drum. On the 2,500 foot summit of that mountain is a fine example, as there is on the top of its neighbour Drosgl, while yet another lies on the ridge between. A gold ornament was said to have been found in this one during the eighteenth century, giving it the name of Carnedd y Ddelw, 'cairn of the image'. This type of discovery illustrates why the cairns may be described as 'robbed' (though this term also refers to the taking of their stones to make nearby walls). Indeed a robber's pit frequently – in fact almost always – indents their summits. One of the hazards of burying treasure with the dead is that people will try to dig it up again – depriving us in the present of much that the grave goods could have told us about the way of life of the people who built the cairns.

Several of the upland cairns (such as that on Drosgl, and that on Moel Wnion, south of Aber) have been adapted to serve as shelters for sheep.

However, where the shape of the cairn has remained sufficiently undisturbed for it to be treated as original, it has been found that a cist (a chest of stone) lies at its centre, signifying its purpose – usually the single burial of cremated dead. The cairn known as **Barclodiad y Gawres**, on the Roman road running through Bwlch y Ddeufaen, has a still-visible cist, eight foot long by about four wide, though some of its side stones have fallen. The name of this cairn, like the one in Anglesey, derives from a story of a giant and giantess carrying stones for the construction of a house. In this case they were on their way to Anglesey through this natural pass. The giant was carrying the two large stones which give the pass its name, while the giantess carried the pile of stones in her apron. Disheartened by the news of how far they had to go they cast down their burdens.

Another cairn in which the central chest may still be seen is that known as **Carnedd y Saeson**, 'the Englishman's cairn', which lies on the slopes of the Anafon valley, among the group already referred to, not far from the Roman road at its Aber end. Several other cairns lie near the route of the road in this direction, providing reason to suppose that this was, long before, an ancient trackway.

The highest cairn in this area, second only to that on Snowdon, lies at 3,484 feet, on the summit of **Carnedd Llywelyn.** It is partly hollowed out in the middle to form a shelter, perhaps intended for sheep but often welcomed by walkers. Next in height is the one on Carnedd Llywelyn's pair, **Carnedd Dafydd**, at 3426 feet, which is actually larger and more imposing.

These summit features owe their existence to the nearby presence of plentiful stones. No doubt the builders made use of the strip of lateral moraine which the now difficult to imagine ice deposited often just below the summit peak. These moraines are largely composed of portable stones and may be moved quite swiftly up a steep slope by means of a human chain. From personal experience I can say that some twenty people can construct a respectable summit cairn in about four hours.

Where stone was not so readily available, the people of the Bronze Age built their burial mounds of earth, indicating that in these cases it was the mound itself, and not its structure, which was significant. These earth mounds or barrows, marked as 'tumulus' on the map, are plentiful in the uplands between Colwyn Bay and Pentrefoelas, indication perhaps that an ancient trackway ran this way across the Denbighshire hills. Three may be seen quite clearly on a ridge known as **Mwdwl Eithin**, which lies about halfway between Llangernyw and Eglwysbach. Of these, the central one was excavated in 1912 by Willoughby

Gardner. It revealed a central cremation and two other cremation burials, one in an urn by then much broken. This evidence helps to link the earth barrows with the stone cairns.

FIVE

STONE AGE AND BRONZE AGE TIMES

In the winter of 1850 a storm stripped the turf from a dune at the side of the Bay of Skaiff, on Mainland Orkney. What it exposed has brought us directly into touch with the way of life of the people who built the cromlechs.

Several things about Skara Brae seem now very odd. One of these is that what came to light first was not a structure at all but a vast rubbish dump, known to archaeologists as the midden. This was a compost heap composed of a mixture of organic material, bones, stone and shells. It had formed into a dense sort of clay.

On investigation, it turned out that the people of Skara Brae lived inside this mound. In it were houses and passages which, their roofs above the midden gone, had filled up with sand.

It was fortunate that the laird of Skaill, who made this extraordinary discovery, had an interest in archaeology, a study which was developing by then into a serious science. Skara Brae was excavated in the 1860's, although it was not until the late 1920's that the full extent of the village was appreciated, after a further storm had removed more of the mound.

Skara Brae is on the edge of the sea now – hence the storm-damage – but when it was inhabited it was in farmland, and the sea lay some way distant. It consists of a number of huts which are one-room dwellings, suitable for housing a nuclear family. These are grouped together in a honeycomb form, with a narrow low-roofed passage twining among them, linking them up. One of the less surprising traits of the inhabitants becomes apparent at once: they were obsessed with keeping out drafts. The passages turn, rather than approaching doorways directly, and are inconveniently low and narrow. The people who lived here were shorter than us, but not so much that they would be able to walk upright along these tunnels. Though the idea of the midden – that you should choose to live inside your rubbish – is strange to us it makes sense from this point of view: rubbish makes an ideal insulating material.

Even bearing in mind this practical aspect, two things are surprising. One is that these people chose to lived packed so tightly together. The second, in contradiction, is that they nevertheless lived in private, separated spaces. Each dwelling had a doorway which could be securely closed. There are no communal living areas, only these private houses.

However, the feature that confronts us most directly with the minds of these people living here 5,000 years ago, is the remarkable consistency of their houses. Like flats in a tower-block, they are all exactly the same. The hearth occupies the centre of the room, and either side of it there are stone-built beds, against the walls. There are storage spaces in the form of cavities set into the walls above the beds. Opposite the door in every case, beyond the hearth, is an item of furniture in a very distinct style. It is known as the dresser, and consists of a set of shelves. Because of its conspicuous position it is thought to be for the purpose of display. What is hard to imagine (in a culture in which people are keen to emphasise the individuality of their houses) is why each householder of Skara Brae felt the need to have a set of shelves in the same position and built in exactly the same style.

The evident emphasis on storage space – the houses have other areas set aside for this purpose, set and built into the walls – tells us something important about them, and their lives. They had possessions, whether in the form of mere seasonal surplus or something more permanent. Though they lived in a very definite social group each family had its own. There were, it seems, no communal storage areas. Yet the conformity to convention seems to convey a very communal attitude, in that it points at least to shared beliefs. Why not, we may wonder then, shared corn? Another characteristic of the social life which is indicated by this strict conformity is the complete lack of hierarchy or differentiation. All the houses are the same size. None has any exclusive feature.

What begins to emerge is the mentality of people who were happy to store all the bones of their ancestors in one chamber, disregarding individuality, yet at the same time went to such extraordinary lengths to house them that we cannot doubt the reverence in which they held them.

Skara Brae was inhabited for about 600 years, somewhere between 3,100 and 2,500 BC. An older village lies immediately under the present one, of much the same form, and so one can assume that it belonged to the same people. That they chose to build again on the same spot presumably when their first houses fell into disrepair tells us something, perhaps, about their sense of place. The village is thought to have been home to about twenty families, though it is not certain how much on the seaward side might have been lost, so that this perhaps forms the remains of a larger settlement. How typical it is of the settlements of this time has not yet been possible to determine.

Some other sites have come to light in the Orkney islands – Noltland, on Westray, and Rinyo, on Rousay – which tend to confirm that this means of dwelling, in clustered housing, was normal. At the same time it seems to have been something of an innovation. At an earlier period farmsteads were scattered, as is perhaps shown by the oldest Orkney dwelling, which dates from about 3,700 BC, known as the Knap of Howar, on Papa Westray. Here two connected structures form accommodation and barn, like a medieval long-house. Again there was an unexpectedly long occupation of this single spot, since the Knap of Howar was found to have been occupied for about 900 years.

The climate was warmer then and the people of Orkney grew more crops than they can now. Barley and wheat were their staples, and they had a rich meat and fish diet: beef, lamb, pork, venison, goat; cod, saithe, lobster, crab, mussels, sea urchins, oysters. They also ate whale meat and seal, seabirds and their eggs. They do not seem to have developed the technique of weaving, and so it is presumed they wore skins. Nevertheless there are also leather-working tools, which imply style or fashion, and the enormous number of beads discovered, as well as pendants and pins, indicates an interest in decoration. They made colours out of ground rock, such as red ochre.

This detailed attention to the people of Skara Brae is made because so much is known about them. Before we go on to consider what is known of others of the time elsewhere, and how far this supports the typical character of life on Orkney then (and hence how valuable this insight might be into the minds of distant people) there is an important point to be made about their evident beliefs. For a long time they had buried their dead in communal village mounds, but towards the end of the period of their settled life at Skara Brae they built Maes Howe.

Maes Howe is not just solely an impressive monument that it indicates in itself a new attitude, and, more importantly, a new way of organising social groups. It has certain distinctive features which associate it directly with Newgrange and the other Boyne mounds; and those, we know, have points in common with tombs of the same age in Anglesey. In Maes Howe there is thus proof of a widespread common culture, which connects the Orkney community with the present subject.

Maes Howe is said by Historic Scotland to be the finest chambered tomb in north-west Europe – though one wonders whether their Irish equivalent would agree with them. Plundered in ancient times, most notably by Vikings, by the time it was formally excavated in the nieteenth century it did not have any of its bones in place. Thus it has not been accurately dated, and the given age of 5,000 years ago is inferred partly from its points of resemblance to Newgrange, which has now been carbon dated. For this reason it is not clear which way the spread of influence flowed – Anglesey to Ireland, Ireland to Orkney, or the other way? However, it is safe to assume that that they were all in use about 3,000 BC. The finding of 'grooved ware' (a type of pottery used by the group of early farmers who built tombs like this also at Skara Brae, connects the tomb with the Stone Age village, and so helps to confirm its date, since Skara Brae has been fully carbon-dated.

There is something else that is striking about this connection, and adds another aspect to understanding the mind of Stone Age man. If the turfed-over replica of one of the houses at Skara Brae is at all accurate, it looks so much like the turf-covered mound of Maes Howe that one cannot help thinking that the tomb must have been thought of as a house for the dead, though one that was better built than it would have been for normal domestic use.

Maes Howe is related to the Boyne and Anglesey groups not just in the similarity of structure – the long passage, the central chamber, the corbelled roof. It has another demonstrable connection, at least with Newgrange. At sunset on the winter solstice the sun shines down its passage into the chamber. As at Newgrange it is found now that the last ray hits the back chamber a little off centre, but this is because the earth has shifted slightly on its axis over the course of the 5,000-year period since the tomb's construction. It can be shown in both cases that if this had not occurred, the midwinter sunset would hit the back wall in the middle, or perhaps strike a central pillar in the chamber that has since gone.

It is not necessary to speculate about beliefs in 'the rebirth of the sun', or even to posit a sun-worshipping people. The importance of the pivot of midwinter to a farming people is obvious enough – it is the time you can safely start to draw on your reserves, the time to start the process of the new year going, preparing land for sowing, now that it will be likely that the days will get warmer and longer.

Presumably the passage, normally blocked, could be opened up annually to permit this phenomenon to be seen. The people of that time could not have anticipated the earth's future wobble. One other thing they could not have predicted: that 5,000 years later the whole world would be able to see the solstice sunset entering the chamber on

Historic Scotland's website.

There are other notable burial mounds in Orkney, such as the Tomb of the Eagles on South Ronaldsay, where more than 16,000 bones of various kinds were found, including the remains of at least 342 people – proving, once again, the communal use of these chambers.

A sense, then, of belonging to a group is one of the characteristics that help explain these people and their activities. Finding them clustered in their adjoining huts, we may feel that they were so unlike us that we cannot come to know them. Yet we too, as seen from the outside, have an apparently inexplicable urge to cluster, to live not on our own, for which there is, after all, plenty of room, but within quarrelling distance of the neighbours. It cannot be just for economic reasons that we gather in conurbations, and leave places such as Orkney empty. In the meantime the honeycomb network of almost identical rooms proclaims close sociability, and the intense domesticity of these rooms – in which the whole family lived and slept around a central hearth – exhibits the composition of that society as being of tight family units – each sealed from their neighbours by a bolted door.

To what extent is this detailed information about people living at the same time as those who built the cromlechs confirmed by other sites? In southern England it seems clear that people of this time lived in houses made of wood, turf and hide, all of which have disappeared without leaving any trace. Much of the evidence, in fact, warns against the temptation to see a homogenous culture. While links between Ireland, Orkney and Wales indicate some sort of shared influence, in terms of tomb-building they do not really prove any further common elements. It has been pointed out that a diversity of tomb-styles, for example in Anglesey, points to small and diverse communities. In writing about the Capel Garmon chambered cairn, Grimes suggests that 'the variety of types into which the tombs can be classified is itself an indication that the settlers arrived over a period in small groups, each with their own distinctive characteristics, but sharing a common mode of life in which agriculture was the most important element'.

Another respect in which Skara Brae might be misleading, and for which the Welsh examples provide little evidence, is the evident pacifism of that society, since the site is not defended and no weapons were found. This may be to do with their good fortune in choosing a spot so remote and perhaps not much sought after. Signs of war for this period have been found elsewhere, such as arrowheads in parts of skeletons, and broken skulls, in graves from Wiltshire through Oxfordshire and Gloucestershire right up to Caithness. Fortifications dating to the Late Stone Age have been identified at Crickley Hill in Gloucestershire, dating from about 3,200 BC, and Corn Brea in Cornwall with a 3,800 BC date, also bears signs of attack and destruction.

These slight signs of conflict point to an early development of competition for land. This is hardly surprising. In fact much more in need of explanation is the long period of settlement – six hundred years at Skara Brae, nine hundred at the Knap of Howar. A long time, perhaps, for an early agricultural settlement to be in one place. The building of the tombs itself indicates a long-term settled presence at other sites, and this in turn suggests two things. One is that the communities were more reliant on the farming of livestock than on cereal crops. Pastoralism does not deplete the land in the way arable farming does, since animals give back to the land some of the nutrients they have taken out. Only on those great alluvial plains, such as the Nile valley or the flood-plains of the Indus and the Tigris-Euphrates, where the annual floods replenish the river valleys with fresh topsoil and essential nutrients brought down as silt, can a farming community grow grain year after year without decline. There is little of that in Britain, so that eventually the crops fail. This brings us to the second point. There is a theory that the tombs resulted from deteriorating fertility of the soil, either as an expression of the right of one group to occupy a fertile patch of land, or as a form of supplication to ancestral gods to restore conditions. Yet as Ronald Hutton points out in *The Pagan Religions of the Ancient British Isles*, the tombs could equally have been a celebration of success, a thanksgiving for the harvesting of plenty. In one way or another authorities feel compelled to relate the two peculiarities of these people: they built tombs, and they farmed. It is of course also the case that both activities involve a form of inhumation; the idea of the dead being sown in order to be reborn is still latent in the Christian funeral service, through St Paul's contemplation in 1 Corinthians. The grain cannot come to life again unless it first dies. The dead, like grain, are sown in weakness, raised in power, sown a natural body, raised a spiritual one – and so on.

Bones of animals feature frequently in the middens of this period, as was the case for example of **Bryn yr Hen Bobl.** Yet there were signs of increasing arable crops as well as increased pasture in the pollen analysis marking the phases of construction of **Trefignath.** Whatever the state of their diet we know that the people's health was not as good as one would expect, given their apparently undemanding life-style. The business of farming itself contributed to ailments, and in *The Stonehenge People,* Aubrey Burl points out that osteoarthritis appears as a major affliction for almost the first time among these farming groups. He attributes it to the effect of hauling tree-trunks, ploughing without traction animals, and carrying heavy loads – the curses inherent in the apparent loss of the innocence of hunting and gathering.

Many other ailments afflicted the population. Ronald Hutton remarks that "their skeletons reveal traces of almost every complaint which can leave a mark upon bone": polio, sinusitis, tetanus, tuberculosis, arthritis, spina bifida, tooth abscesses. Most of them died before they were thirty. Many children, in fact, died before they were seven.

It is agreed that there is considerable consistency about the people's physical characteristics. Enough of them have been found complete for us to be able to generalise. The men were from five foot four to five foot eight in height, the women from five foot to five foot five – in other words only a few inches below the modern average. Their skulls were consistently long and narrow. They had moderately sloping, straight and broad foreheads. Their faces were medium in length and also in width, and a distinguishing characteristic was an exceptionally narrow set of nostrils.

Their short lives evidently kept down the natural increase in their numbers. During the Mid Stone Age, before the time of tomb-building dealting with here, it is estimated that the population of England and Wales was only about 10,000 people. A vast increase must have taken place during the subsequent thousand years, to judge only by the megaliths they left. Aubrey Burl, concerned with the population of Salisbury Plain at the time, shows that a modest 1.002 per cent rise in population (which he shows to be likely at the time) would give rise to a seven-fold increase over a thousand years. This, he points out, would lead to a problem confronting 'any society occupying so small an area as Salisbury Plain'; and this may similarly be applied to Anglesey.

Apart from farming, a little is known of what the population did. They needed a hard stone to make axes, because they needed sharp axes to fell trees. Hence in some parts of Britain they mined flint, following the seams of it through other rock with some noticeable skill. But there was a rock, they discovered, even stronger than flint: the augite granophyre of Penmaenmawr, which is now usually mistakenly called granite. An igneous rock, owing its presence to the fact that Penmaenmawr is a volcanic plug, it burst through the later shale in intrusions around the now destroyed summit. It is a doubly useful rock, for those in need of durable stone tools. The even distribution of its crystals gives it a hardness and a durability, while at the same time it is easily worked by means of flaking. It is of considerable interest to realise that Neolithic man recognised a good thing when he saw one.

The stone axe industrial site – more than just a factory – at Graig Lwyd, above the present town of Penmaenmawr, extended for over two miles, occurring at three separate areas. It was the third largest quarry in Neolithic Britain, but the evidence is that it was the most successful and its products the most sought after. Penmaenmawr stone is easily identified, because of its crystals, which may be observed by microscopic analysis, and the axes from Graig Lwyd have been found not just all over Wales but all over

Britain, and even indeed in Northern Ireland. They occur around the coast, along the Solent and at the far tip of Cornwall, as far north as the Firth of Forth, and up the rivers Severn and Avon.

These quarries produced light axes, which were for local use, and heavy axes for forest clearance, which were exported. The sites of their production have been identified by the presence of the waste flakes and by abandoned axes, often broken or flawed. This evidence reveals how they were made. A block is selected from the scree or hacked off the crags. It is first roughly flaked to reduce its size to manageable form. Then it is further flaked into a regular shape, by means of the use of a heavy beach-stone hammer (some worn-out specimens of which have also been found).

No polished axes were found on site, indicating that once the item was of the right shape and size it was taken elsewhere to be finished. It is apparent that they were usually finished before being transported, since only a few roughouts have been found at any distance.

All this activity went on for several hundred years, and was flourishing in about 2,500 BC. Of course, this reveals a great deal about these people. Not only were they canny and deftly skilled, but they also had an extensive marketing system, and with that inevitably came the exposure to lines of influence and information. This engagement in trade implies a high degree of social and political organisation, as well as a basic knowledge of navigation. Frances Lynch points out that the great distances over which axes were transported indicates that 'well-established trade routes must have existed'.

Older than Graig Lwyd, but never by any means as successful, was the stone axe factory on Mynydd Rhiw, far down the Llŷn peninsula. Here the rock is not igneous, but rather a type of hard shale, and in this case it was not simply quarried but mined. A series of five pits were sunk across this seam of suitable shale. As these were abandoned when they grew too deep, the waste from the next was put into and around them, giving hollows where the working of the tools took place. Only some twenty axes from Mynydd Rhiw have been found, and none further away than Gwent. It indicates however, that industry and trade were factors in several communities at the time of the building of the tombs.

These activities of industry and trade may well help to explain how it happened that the tomb-building in Wales seems to have been influenced from several directions, not just from Ireland but most notably from the area of Neolithic activity which gave rise to the monuments known as the Cotswold-Severn group.

That set of tombs, which is identified by its distinctive style, possibly originated around the Bristol Channel, and is perhaps due to arrivals, perhaps from France. Its distribution occurs mainly on a band from south Wales to the Mendips and the Cotswolds. It is a type commonly known as 'long barrows', and the style shows a notable emphasis on the barrow itself, measuring an average of 150 foot in length and an average of 65" wide. As such these were much more than just a covering for the chamber, or chambers. The good example at West Kennett is however much bigger.

The Cotswold-Severn barrow is typically long and wedge-shaped, with a forecourt set into the wider end. Sometimes it covers a chamber with side-cells, and some of the tombs turn out (like that at **Capel Garmon** in the

Dyffryn Conwy) to have false entrances at the base of the forecourt, the chamber being entered from the side. The form developed early, perhaps during the Mid Neolithic, by about 3,800 BC, and it then spread widely during the fourth millennium.

During the next millennium something radical about the business of tomb-building changed. Sometimes this is seen as a result of the tomb-building programme itself. The construction of such vast monuments, this theory suggests, had proved in the end too big a drain on the fragile economy. The construction of the Orkney monuments, for instance, is estimated to have taken 150,000 man-hours. One estimate reckons the building of each major tomb to have taken up 10,000 man-hours. That this expenditure may have been at the cost of investment in farming is perhaps supported by the evidence of the pollen analysis, since towards the end of the period of tomb construction it shows the forest to be regenerating, and fields which once grew corn were then reverting to scrub.

This trend towards the building of major structures moreover points to several changes which must at that same time have taken place. Such a large-scale programme of civil engineering involved a regional rather than a purely local organisation of the workforce, which must have meant an end, one way or another, to the more intimate family groups. Ideas of hierarchy, then, and of status, were evidently already developing during the last phases of the New Stone Age. This may be seen in terms of an existing population changing, changing in terms of its social values and its skills; or it may, as has often been done, be seen as the arrival of a new one, in due course bearing the knowledge of the use of bronze.

Which of these attitudes is adopted has proved to be largely a matter of academic fashion. Ronald Hutton usefully points out, however, that there is no compulsion to see the arrival of new tools and habits as an indication of the arrival of new people. He observed:

The problem is that an existing population can adopt foreign artefacts and fashions so completely as to appear to have been replaced by foreigners. Thus, according to traditional archaeological practice, had modern Britain been an illiterate society then it would have been natural to have spoken of the invasion of the 'Washing Machine People' in the 1950's and large-scale Japanese immigration in the 1970's.

Bearing this apt warning in mind, the introduction of the vessels known to archaeologists as beakers, found everywhere among the burials after about 2,000 BC, does not compel us to think of the arrival of 'the Beaker people'. This pottery is found all over Europe, and its design could easily have spread over time to the British Isles. There were plenty of other factors of change which do not need to be seen as accompanied by migration. For one thing, the climate was changing. During the last phases of the New Stone Age the weather had been deteriorating slowly. It had been getting cooler and wetter. From about 2,200 BC, however, this trend was reversed. At about the start of the Bronze Age Britain's climate started to get warmer and sunnier, finer in fact than it is today, providing ideal grazing conditions that help to explain the emphasis that emerged on cattle-herding and the encouragement which that gave to greater mobility.

This enabled habitation at greater heights, above the forest level, and it seems to have led to a noticeable change in population distribution. There is, for the first time, a movement away from the coast. Other significant trends have already been noted: burial is now of individuals not groups, often cremated, buried in small stone chests rather than great chambers, and with grave-goods accompanying them; these were often of value, and now included weapons such as arrows (suggesting decayed bows), wristguards, daggers and battle axes. It seems that farming, with its outcome of competition for land, had finally led to a loss of innocence.

In the transition from cromlechs to cairns several factors combine to give perhaps a rather weighted view of the people concerned. To be precise: we know more of the contents of their tombs because more of them remained intact. The need for reopening of communal tombs made them easier to rob, a weakness exacerbated by their location at lower altitudes than the cairns. Moreover the chambers were always associated with cultivated land. Nevertheless those unrobbed chamber tombs which were investigated did not yield these sorts of goods.

Such radical innovations do inevitably tempt us to see these as newly arrived people, and some support for that idea is given by their physical remains. They had rounder skulls than their predecessors, were broader and more heavily built, and although those who wish to resist the immigration theory insist that round skulls were not unknown in Britain before and anyway became dominant slowly over a long period, there does seem to be a possible statistical reason for viewing them as newcomers. It was Professor Gordon Childe, writing in *Prehistoric*

Communities of the British Isles in 1940, who was largely responsible for popularising the notion, which actually dates back to the start of the twentieth century, of these people as being 'warlike invaders'. More recently Frances Lynch has observed, this time in *Prehistoric Wales*, that 'the idea of large-scale introductions of new peoples into Wales or into Britain has been abandoned' – though even that, one feels, might be a simplification.

Assertions on subjects such as this need constant qualification, and it is worth remembering that if indeed they came, bringing their beakers, they do not seem initially to have also brought the use of bronze. That followed them, since the beakers occur first, somewhat before 2,500 BC, and the use of bronze a little after that date. It is, however, for their bronze production that they became best known.

The manufacture of bronze requires the mining of copper. This took place in vast quantities over a long period on the Great Orme. This major industry has in fact a great deal to tell us about these people.

The Great Orme mines date to the period immediately after the Late Neolithic, and so signal a new approach to the making of artefacts. The largest prehistoric mines in Europe, these amount to a major industrial site. The seams were picked with bone tools and the rock around them cracked with beach-stone hammers. By these means tens of thousands of tons of ore were extracted over the 1200 years or so of the mines' prehistoric use.

Here there are two revealing pieces of evidence. First, this is much more copper than could have been needed to make the amount of bronze tools we can estimate that Britain may have possessed during this period; there must, then, have been a related export trade. Secondly, copper on its own is of little use, being too soft to use by itself for tools or weapons. It has to be mixed with tin to make the harder alloy bronze. There is no tin in Wales. The nearest tin mines are in Cornwall.

This reveals an enormous amount. We know that the times were sufficiently stable to permit the transport of valuable metal. We know that the people then were sophisticated enough to have worked out a trading mechanism, by which the ores of copper and tin could be brought together by their respective owners, and foundries set up to manufacture the compound. We know that they were enterprising enough to have developed an intentional surplus of metal production, and then to have set up a marketing system for benefiting from it. We know therefore that we are looking at a high degree of social, political and economic organisation.

Another great source of copper in northern Wales has always been Parys Mountain, in Anglesey, and recent excavation has dated the debris of older mining to almost four thousand years before the present, meaning that this too was in production during the early Bronze Age.

All this advanced civilisation did not seem to have done the people a great deal of good. They were not a healthy lot. Like their predecessors in the Late Stone Age they suffered from arthritis, and some remains have shown signs of malnutrition. Their teeth were terrible, and they had severe back problems. Half of the men died before they were 36, and the women, surprisingly, younger than that. Aubrey Burl reports that a study in Scotland showed that 85 percent of the women died before the age of 25, probably mainly in childbirth.

In spite of these hard conditions they retained an eye for

decoration. They twisted cords around their trade-mark beakers while the clay was wet, to give a characteristic pattern. Out of those beakers they drank some kind of alcohol, probably a type of beer, or mead.

These people, or their way of life, spread fast once it was established. Occurring first in the east of the country, their styles spread rapidly to cover virtually the whole of Britain during the next thousand years. Horse bones found at some of their burial sites have tempted some to speculate that their spread was facilitated by riding. No elements of harness have been found, however, from this particular period, and although Aubrey Burl speculates that this may have been because it perished, there are harness in parts in burials at later periods.

The presence of weapons in their graves, meaning that these were valued, has led several authorities to view the people of this period as warriors. Certainly it is to this era throughout Europe that the roots of the heroic tradition may be traced, as exemplified for instance by the *Iliad*, by the Irish Mythological Cycle, and perhaps by the more mysterious parts of the 'Four Branches' of our own *Mabinogi*.

They erected, along with the great cairns, the standing stones which still so defiantly challenge our understanding on our hillsides, and some elements of the stone circles. One thing that is certain is that they had an interest in leaving a mark on this land. In this they clearly had a motive in common with their immediate forebears.

It was a long time ago, yet the evidence is still all here, within our reach. What you see at first is stones, and stones are themselves unyielding, giving nothing back. But look closer. Beyond the stones one can see the minds and attitudes of the people who put them there. If it was possible to ask them 'Why did you go to so much trouble?' it would not be surprising if they answered with human irrationality, 'Because we could.' It was an extreme way of leaving their mark, but as such it was a symptom of our shared yearning for immortality.

What they convey, these stones, is something else which no doubt formed a motive for their construction. They communicate to us a message from their builders: 'This is our patch, our place, the bit of the world we belong to. We may ancestrally have come from a long way away, but this is the spot which has become home.' The sense of place and of belonging, marked by the stored bones of your ancestors who found it, and the feeling that this connection ought to be for ever, in defence of which idea you leave a mark, so that nobody should ever doubt that commitment, is reminiscent of that involvement which we know by the Welsh word *cynefin*.

BIBLIOGRAPHY

ASHMORE, Patrick: *Maes Howe*, Historic Scotland, 1989.

BUDGE, Sir Wallis: *Egyptian Religion*, Bell, 1959.

BURL, Aubrey: *The Stonehenge People*, BCA, 1987.

CHILDE, V. G.: *Prehistoric Communities of the British Isles*, Chambers, 1940.

CLARKE, David, and MAGUIRE, Patrick: *Skara Brae*, Historic Scotland, 2000.

COE, Michael D.: *The Maya*, Penguin, 1971.

DANIEL, Glyn: *The Megalith Builders of Western Europe*, Penguin, 1963.
The Prehistoric Chamber Tombs of England and Wales, Cambridge University Press, 1950.

FOX, Sir Cyril: *Life and Death in the Bronze Age*, Routledge and Kegan Paul, 1959.

GRANT, Michael (trs.& ed.): *Tacitus; The Annals of Imperial Rome*, Penguin, 1987.

GRIMES, W.F.: *The Megalithic Monuments of Wales*, Proceedings of the Prehistoric Society, 1936. Pp.106-39.
Capel Garmon Chambered Long Cairn, HMSO, 1958.

HALHED, W. B.: *The Maen Pebyll, Mynydd Hiraethog, Denbighshire*, Archeologica Cambrensis, April 1909.

HUTTON, Ronald: *The Pagan Religions of the Ancient British Isles*, BCA, 1991.

LYNCH, Frances, *Prehistoric Anglesey, The Anglesey Antiquarian Society*, 1970.
Megalithic Tombs and Long Barrows in Britain, Shire Books, 1997.
Prehistoric Wales, Sutton Publishing, 2000.
A Guide to Ancient and Historic Wales: Gwynedd, Cadw, 2001.

RIEU, E.V. (ed. & trs.): *The Iliad,* Penguin 1975.
The Odyssey, Penguin 1971.

SANDARS, N.K.: (ed. & trs.) *The Epic of Gilgamesh,*
Penguin, 1972.

SMITH, C. A., and LYNCH, F. M.: *Trefignath and Din
Dryfol: the Excavation of Two Megalithic Tombs in
Anglesey,* Cambrian Archaeological Association
Monograph 3, Cardiff, 1987.

SWANTON, Michael (ed. & trs.): *Beowulf*, Manchester
University Press, 1982.

WACE, Helen, *Mycenae Guide,* Meriden Gravure Co.,
Connecticut, U.S.A., 1963.

WADDY, C. (trs.) *A Viking Cremation-Ceremony,*
Antiquity, March 1934, Vol. VIII

ACKNOWLEDGEMENTS

Inevitably a book such as this makes use of past work done by others, and readers will have become aware that I have been greatly helped in my research by reference to better authorities. In particular I am indebted to the works of Frances Lynch, whom I should also like to thank for her personal advice.

As ever I am grateful to the staff at Conwy library for their patient diligence in tracking down for me often fairly obscure academic works.

Also by the same author

£5.95

£5.50

£5.50

£5.50

History Guides by Michael Senior

MEIRIONNYDD'S STORY
£1.95

THE CROSSING OF THE CONWY
£3.75

LLYS HELIG AND THE MYTH OF LOST LANDS
£4.50

DID LEWIS CARROLL VISIT LLANDUDNO?
£3.50

PORTRAIT OF NORTH WALES
£6.90

NORTH WALES IN THE MAKING
£6.50 – Soft cover £9.75 – hard cover

DID PRINCE MADOC DISCOVER AMERICA?
£5.50

GODS AND HEROES IN NORTH WALES –
A MYTHOLOGICAL GUIDE
£3.25

BACK FROM CATRAETH
£4.50

BRANCH	DATE
RD	2/07